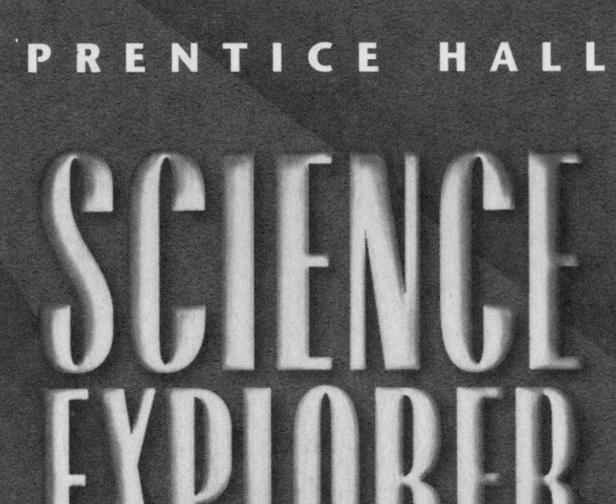

Focus on Physical Science

Student Edition

Guided Reading and Study Workbook

PRENTICE HALL
Needham, Massachusetts
Upper Saddle River, New Jersey
Glenview, Illinois

Student Edition ISBN 0-13-052729-7
1 2 3 4 5 6 7 8 9 10 06 05 04 03 02 01 00

Table of Contents

Chapter 1 Motion

1–1 Describing and Measuring Motion 1
1–2 Slow Motion on Planet Earth 3
1–3 Acceleration 5

Chapter 2 Forces

2–1 The Nature of Force 11
2–2 Force, Mass, and Acceleration 14
2–3 Friction and Gravity 15
2–4 Action and Reaction 18
2–5 Orbiting Satellites 21

Chapter 3 Forces in Fluids

3–1 Pressure 25
3–2 Transmitting Pressure in a Fluid 28
3–3 Floating and Sinking 30
3–4 Applying Bernoulli's Principle 32

Chapter 4 Work and Machines

4–1 What Is Work? 37
4–2 Mechanical Advantage and Efficiency . .39
4–3 Simple Machines 41
4–4 Machines in the Human Body 45

Chapter 5 Energy and Power

5–1 The Nature of Energy 49
5–2 Energy Conversion and Conservation . .51
5–3 Energy Conversions and Fossil Fuels . . .54
5–4 Power 55

Chapter 6 Thermal Energy and Heat

6–1 Temperature and Thermal Energy 59
6–2 The Nature of Heat 61
6–3 Thermal Energy and States of Matter . . .64
6–4 Uses of Heat 67

Chapter 7 Characteristics of Waves

7–1 What Are Waves? 71
7–2 Properties of Waves 73
7–3 Interactions of Waves 76
7–4 Seismic Waves 80

Chapter 8 Sound

8–1 The Nature of Sound 85
8–2 Properties of Sound 87
8–3 Combining Sound Waves 89
8–4 How You Hear Sound 92
8–5 Applications of Sound 93

Chapter 9 The Electromagnetic Spectrum

9–1 The Nature of Electromagnetic Waves . .97
9–2 Waves of the Electromagnetic Spectrum 99
9–3 Producing Visible Light 102
9–4 Wireless Communication 105

Chapter 10 Light

10–1 Reflection and Mirrors 109
10–2 Refraction and Lenses 111
10–3 Color 113
10–4 Seeing Light 115
10–5 Using Light 117

Chapter 11 Magnetism and Electromagnetism

11–1 The Nature of Magnetism 121
11–2 Magnetic Earth 125
11–3 Electric Current and Magnetic Fields . .127
11–4 Electromagnets 130

Chapter 12 Electric Charges and Current

12–1 Electric Charge and Static Electricity . .133
12–2 Circuit Measurements 136
12–3 Series and Parallel Circuits 138
12–4 Electrical Safety 140

Chapter 13 Electricity and Magnetism at Work

13–1 Electricity, Magnetism, and Motion . . .145
13–2 Generating Electric Current 146
13–3 Using Electric Power 150
13–4 Batteries 153

Chapter 14 An Introduction to Matter

14–1 Describing Matter 157
14–2 Measuring Matter 161
14–3 Particles of Matter 163
14–4 Elements From Earth 164

Chapter 15 Changes in Matter

15–1 Solids, Liquids, and Gases 169
15–2 Behavior of Gases 171
15–3 Graphing Gas Behavior 173
15–4 Physical and Chemical Changes 176

TABLE OF CONTENTS *(continued)*

Chapter 16 Elements and the Periodic Table

16–1 Organizing the Elements 181
16–2 Metals 184
16–3 Nonmetals and Metalloids 187
16–4 Elements From Stardust 190

Chapter 17 Chemical Reactions

17–1 Matter and Its Changes 193
17–2 Describing Chemical Reactions 195
17–3 Controlling Chemical Reactions 199
17–4 Fire and Fire Safety 201

Chapter 18 Atoms and Bonding

18–1 Inside an Atom 205
18–2 Atoms in the Periodic Table 207
18–3 Ionic Bonds 209
18–4 Covalent Bonds 212
18–5 Crystal Chemistry 214

Chapter 19 Acids, Bases, and Solutions

19–1 Working With Solutions 217
19–2 Describing Acids and Bases 220
19–3 Acids and Bases in Solution 223
19–4 Digestion and pH 226

Chapter 20 Exploring Materials

20–1 Polymers and Composites 229
20–2 Metals and Alloys 232
20–3 Ceramics and Glass 235
20–4 Radioactive Elements 236

Chapter 21 Chemistry of Living Systems

21–1 Chemical Bonding, Carbon Style 241
21–2 Carbon Compounds 242
21–3 Life With Carbon 246

Chapter 22 Earth, Moon, and Sun

22–1 Earth in Space 251
22–2 Phases, Eclipses, and Tides 253
22–3 Rockets and Satellites 257
22–4 Earth's Moon 259

Chapter 23 The Solar System

23–1 Observing the Solar System 263
23–2 The Sun 266
23–3 The Inner Planets 267
23–4 The Outer Planets 271
23–5 Comets, Asteroids, and Meteors 274
23–6 Is There Life Beyond Earth? 276

Chapter 24 Stars, Galaxies, and the Universe

24–1 Tools of Modern Astronomy 279
24–2 Characteristics of Stars 282
24–3 Lives of Stars 285
24–4 Star Systems and Galaxies 288
24–5 History of the Universe 290

Name ______________________ Date __________ Class ______________

CHAPTER 1

MOTION

SECTION 1-1 Describing and Measuring Motion (pages 6–17)

This section explains how to recognize when an object is in motion and how to determine how fast it is moving.

▶ Recognizing Motion (pages 7–8)

1. An object is in ______________ when its distance from another object is changing.

2. What is a reference point? ______________________________

____

3. An object is in motion if it changes position relative to a(n) __________

______________.

▶ Describing Distance (pages 8–9)

4. Complete the table about SI.

SI	
Question	**Answer**
What is its whole name?	
What number is it based on?	
What is its basic unit of length?	

5. How many centimeters are there in a meter? ______________

6. How many meters are there in a kilometer? ______________

▶ Calculating Speed (pages 10–11)

7. What is the formula used to calculate the speed of an object?

____

8. How would you find the average speed of a cyclist throughout an entire race? ____

____

▶ Describing Velocity (pages 12–15)

9. Speed in a given direction is called _______________.

10. An approaching storm is moving at 15 km/hr. What do you need to know to determine its velocity? ____

____

▶ Graphing Motion (pages 15–17)

11. The steepness, or slant, of a line on a graph is called its _______________.

12. What is the formula used to find the slope of a line?

____

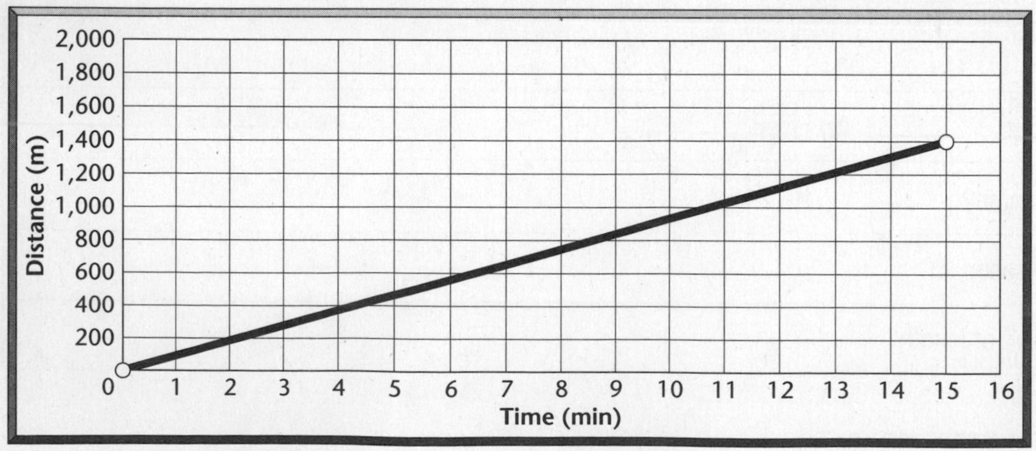

13. The motion graph above graphs the motion of a jogger on a run one day. How far did the jogger run in 15 minutes? _______________

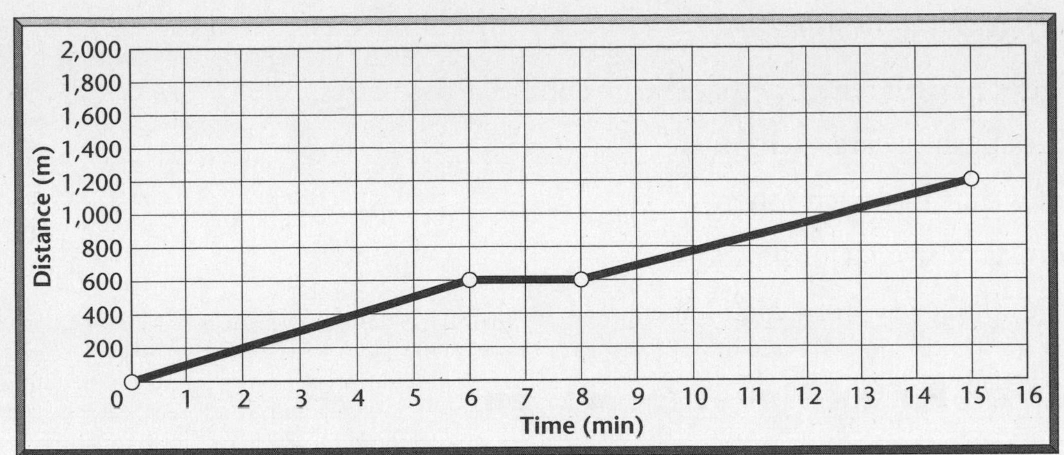

14. The motion graph above also shows the motion of a jogger on a run one day. The line is divided into segments. The middle segment is horizontal. What does that tell you about the jogger's progress between minute 6 and minute 8? ______________________________

____

____

SECTION 1-2 Slow Motion on Planet Earth (pages 20–23)

This section describes the movements of Earth's continents. It also gives a theory that explains why the continents move.

▶ What Are Earth's Plates? (pages 20–21)

1. Is the following sentence true or false? Earth's rocky outer shell is all one piece. ______________
2. The upper layer of Earth consists of more than a dozen major pieces called ______________.
3. What is the theory of plate tectonics? ______________________________

____

____

Name ______________________ Date __________ Class ______________

4. Circle the letter of each sentence that is true about Earth's plates.
   a. Some plates push toward each other.
   b. Some plates slide past each other.
   c. Earth consists of five major plates.
   d. Some plates pull away from each other.

▶ How Fast Do Plates Move? (pages 21–23)

5. Is the following sentence true or false? The speed of Earth's plates is very slow. ______________

6. By knowing the average speed of a plate, what can scientists estimate about Earth's continents? ______________________________

   ____

   ____

7. What formula do scientists use to predict how far a plate will move in a certain amount of time?

   ____

8. Is the following sentence true or false? The shapes and positions of Earth's continents will not change in the future. ______________

9. A conversion factor is a fraction in which the numerator and the denominator are ______________.

Reading Skill Practice

By looking carefully at photographs and illustrations in textbooks, you can help yourself understand what you have read. Look carefully at Figure 10 on pages 22 and 23. What important idea does this illustration communicate? Do your work on a separate sheet of paper.

Name ________________ Date ________ Class ________________

SECTION 1-3

Acceleration
(pages 26-30)

This section describes what happens to the motion of an object as it accelerates, or changes velocity. It also explains how to calculate acceleration.

▶ Acceleration in Science (pages 26–28)

1. What is acceleration? ________________________________

____

2. Acceleration involves a change in what two components?

____

3. Any time the speed of an object increases, the object experiences

________________.

4. Is the following sentence true or false? Acceleration refers to increasing speed, decreasing speed, or changing direction. ________________

5. Deceleration is another word for negative ________________.

6. Is the following sentence true or false? An object can be accelerating even if its speed is constant. ________________

7. Circle the letter of each sentence that describes an example of acceleration.

a. A car follows a gentle curve in the road.

b. A batter swings a bat to hit a ball.

c. A truck parked on a hill doesn't move all day.

d. A runner slows down after finishing a race.

8. The moon revolves around Earth at a fairly constant speed. Is the moon accelerating? ________________________________

____

9. Use the table below to compare and contrast the meanings of *acceleration.*

Acceleration	
In Everyday Language	**In Scientific Language**

▶ Calculating Acceleration (pages 28–30)

10. What must you calculate to determine the acceleration of an object?

____

____

11. What is the formula you use to determine acceleration?

____

12. Is the following sentence true or false? To calculate the acceleration of an automobile, you must first subtract the final speed from the initial speed. ______________

13. Circle the letter of each sentence that is true about calculating the acceleration of a moving object.

   a. If an object is moving without changing direction, then its acceleration is the change in its speed during one unit of time.

   b. If an object's speed changes by the same amount during each unit of time, then the acceleration of the object at any time is the same.

   c. To determine the acceleration of an object, you must calculate the change in velocity during only one unit of time.

   d. If an object's acceleration varies, then you can describe only average acceleration.

Name ______________________ Date __________ Class ______________

14. Suppose velocity is measured in kilometers/hour and time is measured in hours. What is the unit of acceleration? ________________

▶ Graphing Acceleration (page 30)

15. If a graph of distance versus time is a straight line, the graph shows a(n) ________________ relationship.

16. If a graph of distance versus time is a curved line, the graph shows a(n) ________________ relationship.

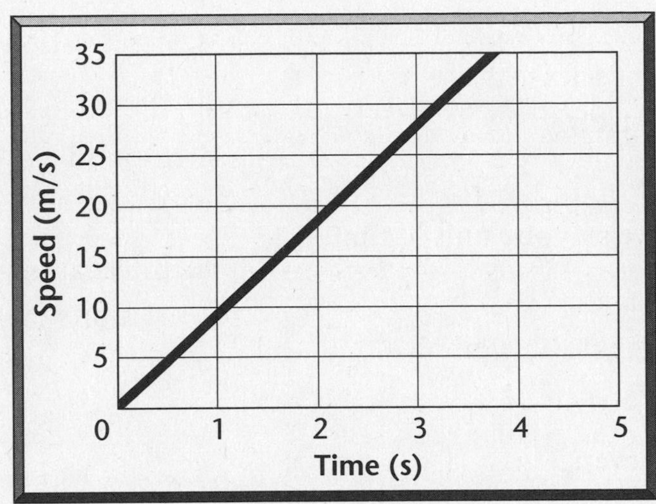

17. The graph above shows the motion of an object that is accelerating. What happens to the speed of the object over time? ________________

____

____

18. The graph line is slanted and straight. What does this line show about the acceleration of the object? ________________________

____

____

WordWise

Match each definition in the left column with the correct term in the right column. Then write the number of each term in the appropriate box below. When you have filled in all the boxes, add up the numbers in each column, row, and two diagonals. All the sums should be the same.

A. When an object's distance from another object is changing

B. A place or object used for comparison to determine if something is in motion

C. The system of measurement scientists use to communicate information clearly

D. The basic SI unit of length

E. The distance an object travels in one unit of time

F. Speed in a given direction

G. The steepness, or slant, of a line on a graph

H. The major pieces of Earth's crust

I. The rate at which velocity changes

1. reference point

2. slope

3. velocity

4. acceleration

5. speed

6. motion

7. meter

8. International System of Units (SI)

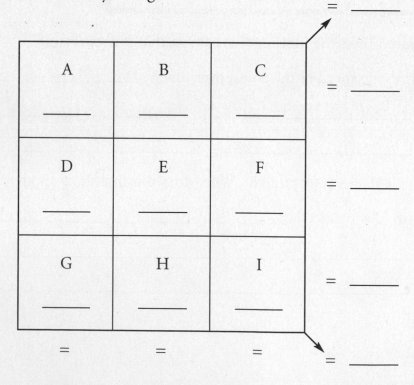

9. plates

			↗ = ____
A ____	B ____	C ____	= ____
D ____	E ____	F ____	= ____
G ____	H ____	I ____	= ____
= ____	= ____	= ____	↘ = ____

Name ______________________ Date __________ Class ______________

MathWise

For the problems below, show your calculations. If you need more space, use another sheet of paper. Write the answers for the problems on the lines below.

▶ Calculating Speed (pages 10–11)

1. $\text{Speed} = \dfrac{32\text{ m}}{8\text{ s}} =$ ______________

2. A car travels 66 kilometers in 3 hours. What is its speed?

Answer: ______________________

▶ Average Speed (page 11)

3. $\text{Average Speed} = \dfrac{200\text{ km}}{5\text{ hr}} =$ ______________

4. Suppose a car travels 60 kilometers the first two hours and 15 kilometers the next hour. What is the car's average speed?

Answer: ______________________

▶ Calculating Slope (page 16)

5. $\text{Slope} = \dfrac{20\text{ m} - 5\text{ m}}{9\text{ s} - 6\text{ s}} =$ ______________

6. A line in a graph has a constant slope. The rise of the line is 15 meters, while the run of the line 3 seconds. What is the slope of the line?

Answer: ______________________

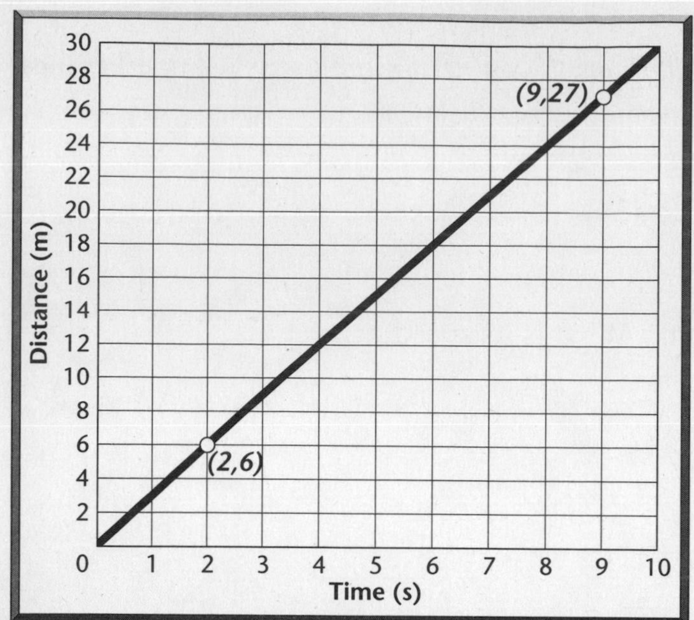

7. Two points on the line graph above are (9, 27) and (2, 6). What is the slope of the line?

Answer: ______________________

▶ Calculating Distance (pages 21–22)

8. Distance $= \frac{7 \text{ cm}}{1 \text{ yr}} \times 1{,}000 \text{ yr} =$ ______________

9. Suppose one of Earth's plates moved 4 cm over the course of a year. How far will it move in 500 years?

Answer: ______________________

▶ Calculating Acceleration (pages 28–30)

11. Acceleration $= \frac{20 \text{ m/s} - 4 \text{ m/s}}{4 \text{ s}} =$ ______________

12. A cheetah accelerates from 2 m/s to 16 m/s in 7 seconds. What is the cheetah's average acceleration?

Answer: ______________________

Name ______________________ Date ________ Class ______________

CHAPTER 2

FORCES

SECTION 2-1

The Nature of Force

(pages 36–41)

This section explains how balanced and unbalanced forces are related to motion. It also explains Newton's first law of motion.

▶ What Is Force? (pages 36–37)

1. In science, a force is ______________________________.

2. When one object pushes or pulls another object, the first object is ______________ a force on the second object.

3. Circle the letters of the two ways that forces are described.

   a. direction b. velocity c. strength d. acceleration

▶ Unbalanced Forces (pages 37–38)

4. When two forces act in the same direction, they ______________ together.

5. Adding a force acting in one direction to a force acting in another direction is the same as adding a(n) ______________ number and a(n) ______________ number.

6. Look at Figure 1 on page 37. What does the width of the arrows tell you about the forces they represent? ______________________________

   ____

7. The overall force on an object after all the forces are added together is called the ______________.

8. The illustrations to the right represent ways that two forces can combine. Draw lines from the left column to the right column to show the result of each combination.

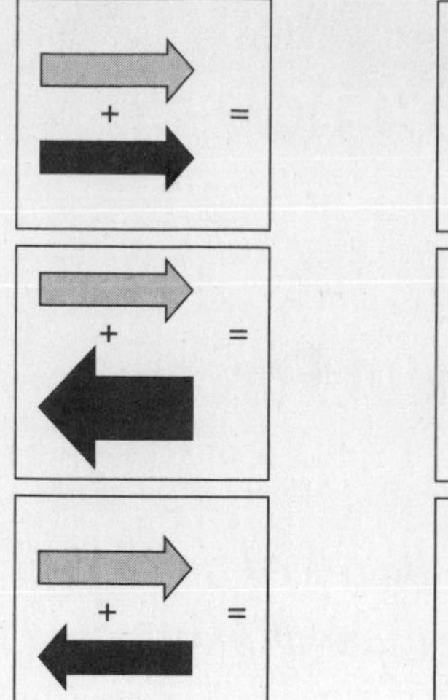

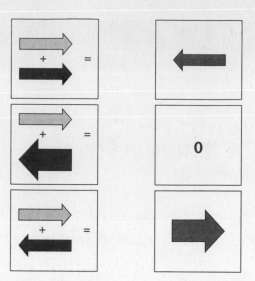

9. Unbalanced forces can cause an object to do three things. What are they?

____

____

10. Is the following sentence true or false? Unbalanced forces acting on an object will change the object's motion. ______________

11. Circle the letter of each sentence that is true about unbalanced forces.
   a. When two forces act in opposite directions, the net force is the difference between the two forces.
   b. When two forces act in the same direction, the net force is the difference between the two forces.
   c. When two forces act in opposite directions, the net force is equal to the greater force.
   d. When two forces act in the same direction, the net force is the sum of the two individual forces.

▶ Balanced Forces (pages 38–39)

12. Equal forces acting on one object in opposite directions are called ______________.

13. Is the following sentence true or false? Balanced forces acting on an object will change the object's motion. _______________

14. When you add equal forces exerted in opposite directions, the net force is _______________.

▶ Newton's First Law of Motion (pages 40–41)

15. For an object to stay in motion, a(n) _______________ has to act on it.

16. Is the following sentence true or false? Once an object is in its natural resting place, it cannot move by itself. _______________

17. What is inertia? _______________

18. What is Newton's first law of motion? _______________

19. Newton's first law of motion is also called the law of _______________.

20. What explains why you continue moving forward if you are in a car that suddenly stops? _______________

21. What is mass? _______________

22. What is the SI unit of mass? _______________

23. The amount of inertia an object has depends on its _______________.

24. How can mass be defined in terms of inertia? _______________

SECTION 2-2 Force, Mass, and Acceleration
(pages 44–46)

This section explains how force and mass are related to acceleration.

▶ Newton's Second Law of Motion (pages 44–45)

1. What is Newton's second law of motion? ______

______

______

______

2. What is the equation that describes the relationship among quantities of force, mass, and acceleration?

______

3. Circle the letters of the two answers below that are different names for the same unit of measure.

a. m/s^2 **b.** N **c.** $kg \cdot ms^2$ **d.** 1 kg

4. What equation for Newton's second law can you use to find acceleration?

______

▶ Changes in Force and Mass (page 46)

5. How does an increase of force affect acceleration? ______

______

______

6. What are two ways you can increase the acceleration of an object?

______

______

7. How does an increase of mass affect acceleration? ______________

____

8. Is the following sentence true or false? One way to increase the force used to pull a wagon is to decrease the mass in the wagon.

____

SECTION 2-3

Friction and Gravity
(pages 47–53)

This section describes the effects of friction on surfaces that rub on each other. It also describes how gravity acts between objects in the universe.

▶ Friction (pages 48–49)

1. Is the following sentence true or false? When two surfaces rub, the irregularities of one surface get caught on those of the other surface.

____

2. What is friction? ______________________________

____

____

3. Friction acts in a direction ______________ to the object's direction of motion.

4. The strength of the force of friction depends on what two factors?

____

____

5. How is friction useful in helping you walk? ______________

____

____

____

6. How does friction help an automobile move? ______________________

____

____

7. Complete the following table about the different kinds of friction.

Kinds of Friction	
Kind of Friction	**Friction Occurs When . . .**
	An object moves through a fluid
	Solid surfaces slide over each other
	An object rolls over a surface

8. Which kind of friction requires more force to overcome, rolling friction or sliding friction? ______________________

9. What kind of friction occurs when moving parts have ball bearings?

____

10. How does oil between machine parts reduce friction? ______________

____

____

▶ Gravity (pages 50–52)

11. The force that pulls objects toward Earth is called ______________.

12. When is an object said to be in free fall? ______________________

____

13. Near the surface of Earth, what is the acceleration of an object due to the force of gravity? ______________

14. An object that is thrown is called a(n) ______________.

15. Is the following sentence true or false? An object that is dropped will hit the ground before an object that is thrown horizontally. ______________

16. Objects falling through air experience a type of fluid friction called ______________________.

17. Is the following sentence true or false? The greater the surface area of an object, the greater the air resistance. ______________

18. On the diagram below, draw arrows that show the forces acting on the falling acorn. Label each arrow with the name of the force.

19. The greatest velocity a falling object reaches is called ______________.

20. What is weight? ____

____

____

21. How is weight different than mass? ______________________________

____

____

____

22. Weight is usually measured in ______________.

▶ Universal Gravitation (pages 52–53)

23. Is the following sentence true or false? The force that makes an apple fall to the ground is the same force that keeps Earth orbiting the sun.

____

24. What does the universal law of gravitation state? _______________

____

____

25. Is the following sentence true or false? On the moon, your mass would be less than it is on Earth, but your weight would be the same.

____

26. The force of attraction between two objects varies with what two factors? _______________

____

SECTION 2-4 Action and Reaction (pages 56–61)

This section explains Newton's third law of motion. It also explains a law about moving objects.

▶ Newton's Third Law of Motion (pages 56–58)

1. What is Newton's third law of motion? _______________

____

____

____

2. What did Newton call the force exerted by the first object on a second object? _______________

Name ______________________ Date __________ Class ______________

3. What did Newton call the force exerted by the second object back on the first object? ______________________

4. The action and reaction forces in any situation will always be ______________ and ______________.

5. Complete the flowchart below, which describes how a squid moves through water.

Newton's Squid

A squid expels water out its back end. This is the ______________ force.
↓
The water expelled out of the back end of the squid pushes back, exerting an equal and ______________ force on the squid. This is the ______________ force.
↓
The squid moves ______________ through the water as a result of the reaction force.

6. Explain why the equal action and reaction forces do not cancel each other when one person hits a ball. ______________________

____

____

____

____

____

▶ Momentum (page 58)

7. The product of an object's mass and velocity is its ________________.

8. What is the equation you use to determine the momentum of an object?

____

9. What is the unit of measurement for momentum? ________________

____

▶ Conservation of Momentum (pages 60–61)

10. What does the law of conservation of momentum state? ____________

____

____

11. Suppose a train car moving down a track at 10 m/s hits another train car that is not moving. Explain how momentum is conserved after the collision. ____

____

____

____

Reading Skill Practice

A flowchart can help you remember the order in which a series of events occurs. Create a flowchart that describes how momentum is conserved when a moving train car collides with another moving train car. See your textbook on page 60. The first step in the flowchart will be this: One train car moves down a track at 10 m/s. The last step in the flowchart will be this: Momentum is conserved. Do your work on a separate sheet of paper. For more information about flowcharts, see page 833 in the Skills Handbook of your textbook.

Name ______________________ Date __________ Class ______________

SECTION 2-5 Orbiting Satellites
(pages 62-64)

This section explains how a rocket lifts off the ground and what keeps an object in orbit.

▶ How Do Rockets Lift Off? (pages 62-63)

1. Which of Newton's laws explains the lifting of a rocket into space?

____

2. When a rocket rises, what causes the action force? ______________

____

____

3. When a rocket rises, what causes the reaction force? ______________

____

____

____

4. On the diagram of a rocket lifting off the ground, draw and label arrows that show the action force and the reaction force.

5. When a rocket lifts off the ground, the net force is in an upward direction. Is the upward pushing force greater or lesser than the downward pull of gravity? ______________

▶ What Is a Satellite? (pages 63–64)

6. Any object that travels around another object in space is a(n) ______________.

7. An object traveling in a circle is accelerating because it is constantly changing ______________.

8. What is a force called that causes an object to move in a circle?

   ____

9. For a satellite, what is the centripetal force that causes it to move in a circle? ______________

10. Is the following sentence true or false? Satellites in orbit around Earth continually fall toward Earth. ______________

11. Explain why a satellite in orbit around Earth does not fall into Earth.

    ____

    ____

    ____

12. A satellite is a projectile that falls ______________ Earth rather than into Earth.

13. Why doesn't a satellite need fuel to keep orbiting? ______________

    ____

    ____

14. What force continually changes a satellite's direction? ______________

Name ______________________ Date __________ Class ______________

WordWise

Use the clues to help you find the key terms from Chapter 2 hidden in the puzzle below. The terms may occur vertically, horizontally, or diagonally.

1. A ________________ is a push or pull.
2. The overall force on an object after all forces are added together is called the ________________ force.
3. The tendency of an object to resist change in its motion is called ________________.
4. The amount of matter in an object is called ________________.
5. One ________________ equals the force required to accelerate 1 kilogram of mass at 1 meter per second per second.
6. The force that one surface exerts on another when the two rub against each other is called ________________.
7. When solid surfaces slide over each other, the kind of friction that occurs is ________________ friction.
8. The friction that occurs when an object moves through a fluid is called ________________ friction.
9. The force that pulls objects toward Earth is ________________.
10. When the only force acting on a falling object is gravity, the object is said to be in ________________ fall.
11. Objects falling through air experience a type of fluid friction called ________________ resistance.
12. The force of gravity on a person or object at the surface of a planet is known as ________________.
13. The ________________ of an object is the product of its mass and velocity.
14. Any object that travels around another object in space is a(n) ________________.

```
m q m o m e n t u m
a f g i n e r t i a
s o r l i o l n g f
s r a i q a z y n r
w c v p c f r e e i
w e i g h t a e w c
u p t f l u i d t t
i e y c n i r o o i
n s l i d i n g n o
s a t e l l i t e n
```

Name ________________ Date ________ Class ________

MathWise

For the problems below, show your calculations. If you need more space, use another sheet of paper. Write the answers for the problems on the lines below.

▶ Newton's Second Law of Motion (pages 44–45)

1. Force = 65 kg × $3ms^2$ = ________________

2. A 250-kg trailer is being pulled by a truck. The force causes the trailer to accelerate at 4 m/s^2. What is the net force that causes this acceleration?

   Answer: ________________

▶ Weight and Mass (pages 51–52)

3. Weight = 45 kg × 9.8 m/s^2 = ________________

4. What is the weight of a rock that has a mass of 7 kg?

   Answer: ________________

▶ Momentum (page 59)

5. Momentum = 5 kg × 6.5 m/s = ________________

6. A baseball travels at 7 m/s, while a basketball moves at 3 m/s. The mass of the baseball is 0.14 kg and the mass of the basketball is 0.5 kg. Which has the greater momentum? ________________

   ____

   ____

Name ______________________ Date __________ Class ______________

CHAPTER 3

Forces in Fluids

SECTION 3-1

Pressure
(pages 70–75)

This section explains what causes pressure in fluids. It also describes how pressure changes with altitude and depth.

▶ What Is Pressure? (pages 70–72)

1. What do snowshoes do that makes it easier for the person wearing them to travel in deep snow? ______________________________

____

____

____

2. Is the following sentence true or false? Force and pressure are the same thing. ______________

3. What is pressure equal to? ______________________________

____

____

4. Circle the letter of the term that is an SI unit of pressure.

a. newton **b.** liter **c.** weight **d.** pascal

5. Circle the letter of the *two* answers below that are equal to each other.

a. 1 Pa **b.** 1 N/cm^2 **c.** 1 N/m^2 **d.** 1 N

6. What unit of measure is used when a smaller unit is more practical for an area? ______________

7. Is the following sentence true or false? You can produce a lower pressure by decreasing the area a force acts on. ______________

▶ Fluid Pressure (page 72)

8. A substance that can easily flow is a(n) ______________.

9. Circle the letter of each of the following that are fluids.

   a. helium gas   b. liquid water   c. ice   d. air

10. Describe how molecules move in fluids. ______________

____

____

____

11. What causes the pressure exerted by a fluid? ______________

____

____

____

12. The pressure exerted by a fluid is the total force exerted by the fluid divided by the ______________ over which the force is exerted.

▶ Fluid Pressure All Around (page 73)

13. What is another term for air pressure? ______________

14. What causes air pressure? ______________

____

▶ Balanced Pressures (pages 73–74)

15. Is the following sentence true or false? In a fluid that is not moving, pressure at a given point is exerted equally in all directions.

____

Name ______________________ Date __________ Class ______________

16. On the illustration of the hand, draw arrows that indicate where the atmosphere is exerting air pressure on the hand. The size of each arrow should indicate the amount of air pressure on that part of the hand.

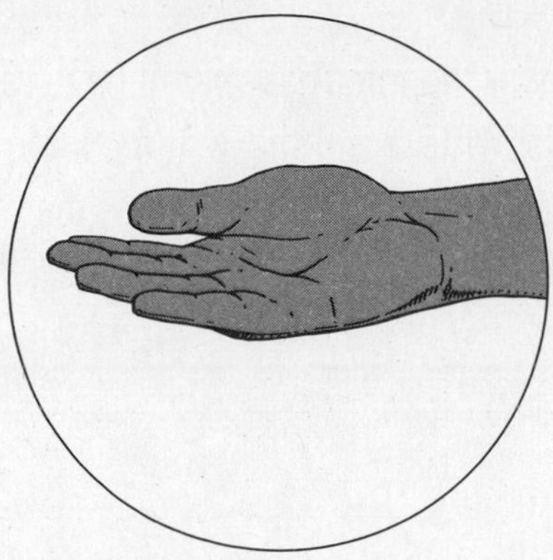

▶ Variations in Fluid Pressure (pages 74–75)

17. Is the following sentence true or false? Air pressure increases as elevation increases. ______________

18. Why is air pressure lower at a higher elevation than at a lower elevation?

____

____

____

____

19. Is the following sentence true or false? Water pressure increases as depth increases. ______________

20. Why is water pressure greater at a greater depth than at a shallow depth?

____

____

____

21. The total pressure at a given point beneath the water results from the weight of the water above plus the weight of the ______________ above it.

Reading Skill Practice

Writing a summary can help you remember the information you have read. When you write a summary, write only the important points. Write a summary of the information under the heading *Fluid Pressure,* page 72. Your summary should be shorter than the text on which it is based. Do your work on a separate sheet of paper.

SECTION 3-2

Transmitting Pressure in a Fluid

(pages 78–81)

This section explains what Pascal's principle says about an increase in fluid pressure and describes how a hydraulic device works.

▶ Pascal's Principle (page 79)

1. What happens to the pressure in a bottle of water if you press the stopper at the top down farther? ______________________

____

____

2. What is the relationship known as Pascal's principle? ______________

____

____

____

▶ Force Pumps (page 79)

3. What does a force pump do? ______________________

____

____

4. Describe the heart in terms of force pumps. ______________________

____

____

▶ Using Pascal's Principle (pages 80–81)

5. Suppose you push down on a small piston that is connected to a confined fluid, and another piston with the same area is connected by a U-shaped tube to the confined fluid. How much fluid pressure will the second piston experience compared to the first? ______________________

____

____

6. Suppose you push down on a small piston that is connected to a confined fluid, and a piston twenty times larger is connected by a U-shaped tube to the confined fluid. How much fluid pressure will the larger piston experience compared to the small piston? ______________

____

7. In a hydraulic system, how is the force applied on a small surface area multiplied? ______________________

____

____

8. Is the following sentence true or false? A car's brake system multiples the force of the driver's tap on the brake pedal. ______________

9. The tube feet of a sea star take advantage of what principle to move around? ______________

10. When a sea star contracts different muscles, it changes the ______________ in the fluid of its tube foot.

11. The ______________ a sea star exerts on the fluid in its system causes the tube foot to either push down or pull up on its sucker.

SECTION 3-3 Floating and Sinking (pages 82-88)

This section describes a force that acts on objects under water. It also explains why some objects float and others sink.

▶ Buoyancy (page 83)

1. Water exerts a(n) ________________ force that acts on a submerged object.

2. Circle the letter of each sentence that is true about a buoyant force.
   a. It acts against the force of gravity.
   b. It acts in an upward direction.
   c. It makes an object feel heavier.
   d. It makes an object feel lighter.

3. How much fluid does a submerged object displace? ________________

   ____

   ____

4. What does the Archimedes' principle state? ________________

   ____

   ____

▶ Floating and Sinking (page 86)

5. Is the following sentence true or false? If the weight of a submerged object is less than the buoyant force, the object will sink.

   ____

6. What happens when the weight of a submerged object is exactly equal to the buoyant force? ________________

   ____

   ____

Name ______________________ Date __________ Class ______________

▶ Density (pages 86–88)

7. The ________________ of a substance, no matter what state or shape, is its mass per unit volume.

8. What formula do you use to find density? ________________________

9. What is the density of water? ________________

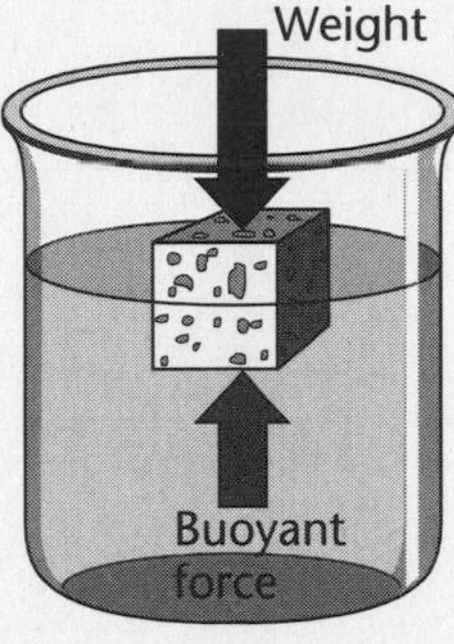

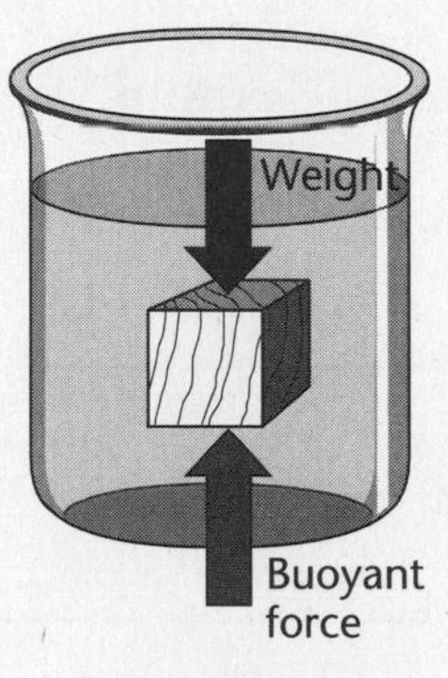

________________ ________________ ________________

10. The illustrations above show three objects in water. All three objects are equal in volume. The captions for these illustrations are listed below. Write the letter of the correct caption under each illustration.

a. Object is more dense than water.

b. Object is less dense than water.

c. Object has a density that is equal to water's density.

11. Is the following sentence true or false? An object that is more dense than the fluid in which it is immersed floats to the surface.

____

12. An object that is ________________ dense than the fluid in which it is immersed sinks.

13. Figure 16 on page 87 shows the densities of several substances. Use the figure to rank the following substances, from 1 for least dense to 3 for most dense.

_____ **a.** corn syrup _____ **b.** wood _____ **c.** plastic

14. Why does a helium balloon rise in air while an ordinary balloon filled with air does not? ________________________________

____

____

____

15. When a submarine pumps water out of its floatation tanks, its density decreases and it floats. Why does its density decrease? ____________

____

____

____

16. Usually, the hull of a ship contains a large volume or air. Why?

____

____

17. The amount of fluid displaced by a submerged object depends on its ______________.

18. A ship stays afloat as long as the ______________ force is greater than its weight.

SECTION 3–4 Applying Bernoulli's Principle (pages 89–92)

This section explains how the pressure of a fluid is related to the motion of the fluid.

▶ Bernoulli's Principle (pages 89–90)

1. Is the following sentence true or false? The faster a fluid moves, the more pressure the fluid exerts. ______________

2. What does Bernoulli's principle state? ______________________

____

____

3. Is the following sentence true or false? A faster-moving fluid exerts less pressure than a slower-moving fluid. ______________

4. Explain why a sheet of tissue paper rises when you blow air above the tissue paper. ______________________

____

____

▶ Objects in Flight (pages 90–91)

5. Is the following sentence true or false? Objects can be designed so that their shapes cause air to move at different speeds above and below them.

____

6. If the air moves faster above an object, does pressure push the object upward or downward? ______________

7. If the air moves faster below an object, does pressure push the object upward or downward? ______________

8. On the illustration of a wing below, draw arrows that show the path of air above and below the wing.

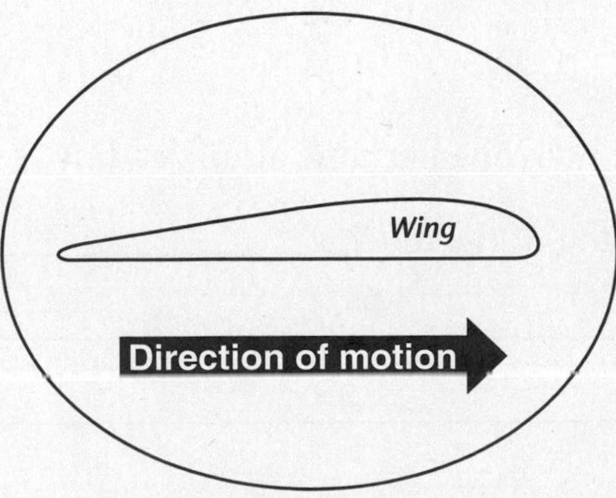

9. Air that moves over the top of an airplane wing must travel farther than air that moves along the bottom of the wing. As a result, the air moving over the top exerts less _______________ than the air moving along the bottom.

10. What is lift? _______________

11. In what way is an airplane wing shaped like a bird's wing? _______________

12. Why is a spoiler on a racing car curved on the lower side? _______________

▶ Bernoulli's Principle at Home (pages 90–92)

13. How do differences in air pressure cause smoke to rise up a chimney?

14. Is the following sentence true or false? The moving water of a shower causes greater air pressure inside the shower curtain than outside the curtain. _______________

15. When you squeeze the rubber bulb of a perfume atomizer, how do you change the air pressure at the top of the tube? _______________

Name ______________________ Date __________ Class ______________

WordWise

Answer the questions by writing the correct key terms in the blanks. Use the circled letter in each term to find the hidden key term. Then write a definition for the hidden key term.

1. Whose principle states that when force is applied to a confined fluid, an increase in pressure is transmitted equally to all parts of the fluid?

◯ _ _ _ _ _

2. What is the force that acts in an upward direction, against the force of gravity, so it makes an object feel lighter?

_ _ _ _ _ _ _   _ _ ◯ _ _

3. What kind of system multiplies by transmitting pressure to another part of a confined fluid?

_ _ _ _ _ _ _ _ _   _ _ _ _ ◯ _

4. What is the unit of pressure equal to N/m^2?

_ _ ◯ _ _ _

5. What is the measurement of how much mass of a substance is contained in a unit of volume?

_ _ _ ◯ _ _ _

6. What is a substance that can easily flow?

_ _ ◯ _ _

7. Whose principle states that the buoyant force on an object is equal to the weight of the fluid displaced by the object?

_ ◯ _ _ _ _ _ _ _ _

8. Whose principle states that the pressure exerted by a moving stream of fluid is less than the pressure of the surrounding fluid?

_ ◯ _ _ _ _ _ _ _

Key Term: _ _ _ _ _ _ _ _

Definition: ____

____

MathWise

For the problems below, show your calculations. If you need more space, use another sheet of paper. Write the answers for the problems on the lines below.

▶ Calculating Pressure (pages 71–72)

1. Pressure $= \dfrac{20\text{ N}}{10\text{ m}^2} =$ ______________

2. A force of 25 N is exerted on a surface with an area of 5 m^2. What is the pressure on that area?

   Answer: ______________

3. A force of 160 N is exerted on a surface with an area of 40 m^2. What is the pressure on that area?

   Answer: ______________

▶ Density (pages 86–87)

4. Density $= \dfrac{12\text{ g}}{3\text{ cm}^3} =$ ______________

5. A substance has a mass of 30 g and a volume of 15 cm^3. What is its density?

   Answer: ______________

6. A substance has a volume of 20 cm^3 and a mass of 10 g. What is its density?

   Answer: ______________

Name ______________________ Date __________ Class __________

CHAPTER 4

WORK AND MACHINES

SECTION 4–1 What Is Work?
(pages 98–101)

This section explains the scientific meaning of work and describes how to calculate the work done on an object.

▶ The Meaning of Work (pages 98–100)

1. In scientific terms, when do you do work? ______________________

____

____

____

2. Complete the following table by classifying each example as either work or no work.

Work?	
Example	**Work or No Work?**
You pull your books out of your book bag.	
You lift a bin of newspapers.	
You push on a car stuck in the snow.	
You hold a heavy piece of wood in place.	
You pull a sled through the snow.	
You hold a bag of groceries.	

3. In order for you to do work on an object, the object must move some

______________ as a result of your force.

4. Explain why you don't do any work when you carry an object at a constant velocity. ____

____

____

____

5. When you pull a sled through the snow, why does only part of your force do work? ____

____

____

____

▶ Calculating Work (pages 100–101)

6. The amount of work you do depends on both the amount of ________________ you exert and the ________________ the object moves.

7. Is the following sentence true or false? Lifting a heavier object demands greater force than lifting a lighter object. ________________

8. Is the following sentence true or false? Moving an object a shorter distance requires more work than moving an object a greater distance.

____

9. What formula do you use to determine the amount of work done on an object? ____

10. What is the SI unit of work? ________________

11. What is the amount of work you do when you exert a force of 1 newton to move an object a distance of 1 meter? ________________

Name ______________________ Date __________ Class __________

SECTION 4–2 Mechanical Advantage and Efficiency

(pages 102–107)

This section explains how machines make work easier and describes how to calculate how efficient a machine is.

▶ What Is a Machine? (pages 102–104)

1. What is a machine? ____

____

____

2. Is the following sentence true or false? A machine decreases the amount of work needed to do a job. ____________

3. Circle the letter of the sentences that are true about how a machine makes work easier.
   - **a.** A machine makes work easier by multiplying force you exert.
   - **b.** A machine makes work easier by reducing the amount of force needed to do the job.
   - **c.** A machine makes work easier by multiplying the distance over which you exert force.
   - **d.** A machine makes work easier by changing the direction in which you exert force.

4. The force you exert on a machine is called the ____________.

5. The force exerted by the machine is called the ____________.

6. Is the following sentence true or false? In some machines, the output force is greater than the input force. ____________

7. If a machine allows you to use less force to do some amount of work, then you must apply the input force over a greater ____________.

8. Is the following sentence true or false? In some machines, the output force is less than the input force. ____________

9. Write labels on the illustration below to show which arrow represents the input force and which represents the output force.

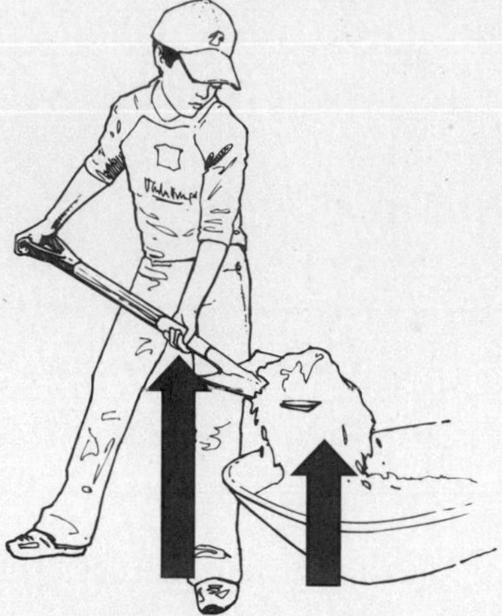

▶ Mechanical Advantage (page 105)

10. What is a machine's mechanical advantage? ______________________

____

____

11. What is the formula you use to determine the mechanical advantage of a machine?

____

12. In a machine that has a mechanical advantage of more than 1, the

______________ force is greater than the ______________ force.

▶ Efficiency of Machines (pages 106–107)

13. In any machine, some work is wasted overcoming ______________.

14. The comparison of a machine's output work to its input work is

______________.

15. What is the formula you use to calculate the efficiency of a machine?

____

16. The mechanical advantage that a machine provides in a real situation is called the ______________ mechanical advantage.

17. The mechanical advantage of a machine without friction is called the machine's ______________ mechanical advantage.

Reading Skill Practice

By looking carefully at photographs and illustrations in textbooks, you can help yourself understand what you have read. Look carefully at Figure 5 on page 103. What important idea does this illustration communicate?

SECTION 4-3

Simple Machines
(pages 110–120)

This section describes the six kinds of simple machines. It also explains how to calculate the advantage of using simple machines.

▶ Introduction (page 110)

1. What are the six basic kinds of simple machines?

   a. ______________ b. ______________ c. ______________

   d. ______________ e. ______________ f. ______________

▶ Inclined Plane (pages 111–112)

2. What is an inclined plane? ______________

3. What formula do you use to determine the ideal mechanical advantage of an inclined plane?

4. Circle the letter of each sentence that is true about inclined planes.

a. The necessary input force is less than the output force.

b. A ramp is an example of an inclined plane.

c. The necessary input force is more than the output force.

d. An inclined plane allows you to exert your force over a longer distance.

5. You can increase the ________________ of an inclined plane by decreasing the friction.

▶ Wedge (page 112)

6. What is a wedge? ____

____

____

7. Is the following sentence true or false? In a wedge, the inclined plane itself moves. ________________

8. Is the following sentence true or false? A wedge multiples force to do the job. ________________

▶ Screws (page 113)

9. What is a screw? ____

____

10. A spiral inclined plane forms the ________________ of a screw.

11. When using a screwdriver to twist a screw into a piece of wood, where is the input force applied and where is the output force exerted?

____

____

____

Name ______________________ Date __________ Class __________

▶ Levers (pages 113–115)

12. What is a lever? ____

____

____

13. The fixed point that a lever pivots around is called the ______________.

14. Circle the letter of each sentence that is true about levers.

   a. A lever increases the effect of your input force.

   b. There are three different types of levers.

   c. A lever changes the direction of your input force.

   d. The fulcrum is always located at the same place on a lever.

15. On each diagram below, draw a triangle below the lever to show where the fulcrum is located on each class of lever.

First-class levers

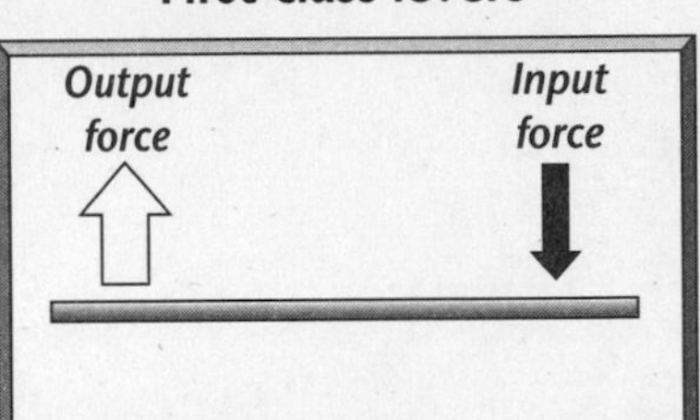

Second-class levers

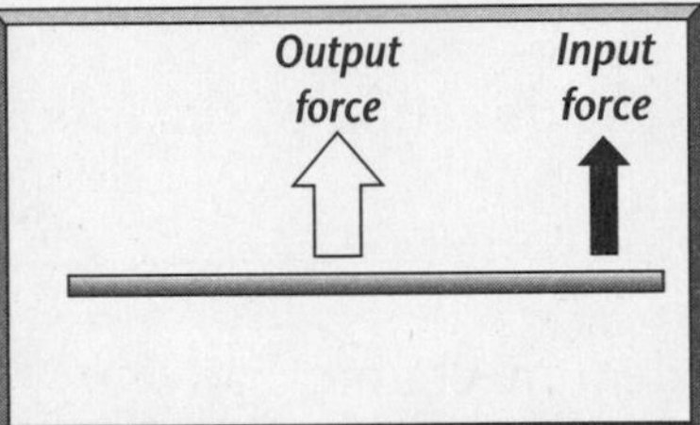

Third-class levers

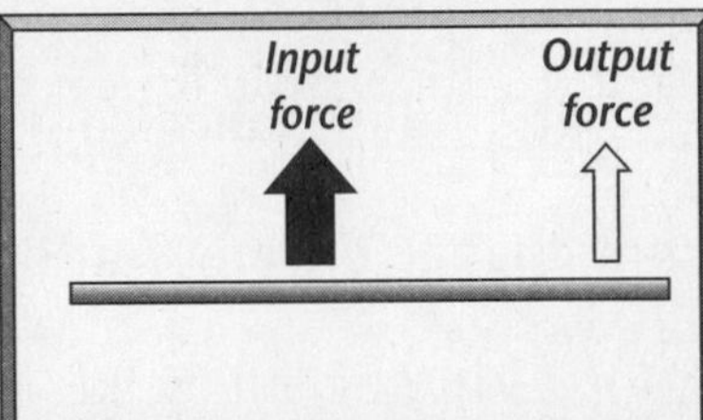

16. Complete the following table about levers.

Levers	
Class of Lever	**Examples**
	Door, wheel barrow, bottle opener
	Seesaw, scissors, pliers
	Baseball bat, shovel, rake

17. What formula do you use to calculate the ideal mechanical advantage of a lever?

____

▶ Wheel and Axle (pages 116–118)

18. What is a wheel and axle? ______________________________

____

____

19. What formula do you use to calculate the ideal mechanical advantage of a wheel and axle?

____

▶ Pulley (pages 118–119)

20. What is a pulley? ______________________________

____

____

21. What kind of pulley changes the direction of the input force but does not change the amount of force you apply? ______________

22. What kind of pulley has an ideal mechanical advantage of 2?

____

▶ Compound Machines (page 120)

23. What is a compound machine? ______________________________

____

24. What do you need to know to calculate the mechanical advantage of a compound machine? ______________________________

____

____

25. A system of ______________ is a device with toothed wheels that fit into one another.

Name ______________________ Date __________ Class ______________

SECTION 4-4 Machines in the Human Body

(pages 124–126)

This section describes how the body uses natural levers and wedges.

▶ Living Levers (pages 124–126)

1. What do most of the levers in your body consist of? ______________________

____

2. Your muscles are attached to your bones by tough connective tissue called ______________.

3. In a living lever in your body, what acts as the lever's fulcrum?

____

____

4. On the illustration of a living lever, label each arrow to show where the input force and the output force are located. Also show where the fulcrum is located.

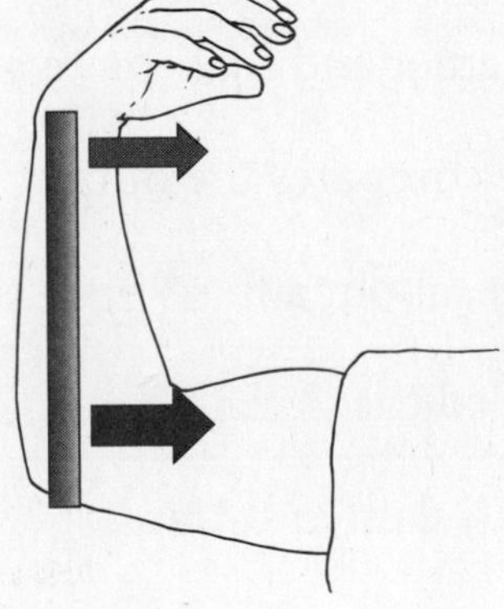

▶ Working Wedges (page 126)

5. What simple machines do your incisors resemble? ______________________

6. Explain how your front teeth are like an ax. ______________________

____

____

____

Name ______________________ Date __________ Class ______________

WordWise

Complete the sentences by using one of the scrambled words below.

Word Bank

lelyup xela oounmpdc fiienycef ttuuop veelr

euojl deegw tupni rwko wecrs clruumf iclndeni enihcam

A device that is thick at one end and tapers to a thin edge at the other end is a(n) ______________.

A machine that utilizes two or more simple machines is called a(n) ______________ machine.

The force exerted by a machine is called the ______________ force.

The fixed point that a lever pivots around is called the ______________.

You do ______________ on an object when you exert a force on the object that causes the object to move some distance.

A wheel and ______________ is a simple machine made of two circular or cylindrical objects that are fastened together and that rotate around a common axis.

The ______________ of a machine compares the output work to the input work.

A rigid bar that is free to pivot, or rotate, about a fixed point is a(n) ______________.

The force you exert on a machine is called the ______________ force.

A(n) ______________ plane is a flat, slanted surface.

A grooved wheel with a rope wrapped around it is a(n) ______________.

A device with which you can do work in a way that is easier or more effective is a(n) ______________.

The SI unit of work is called the ______________.

A(n) ______________ can be thought of as an inclined plane wrapped around a cylinder.

Name ______________________ Date __________ Class ______________

MathWise

For the problems below, show your calculations. If you need more space, use another sheet of paper. Write the answers for the problems on the lines below.

▶ Calculating Work (pages 100–101)

1. Work = 10 N × 35 m = ______________

2. An elevator lifts a man with a weight of 500 N up three floors, or 30 m. How much work did the elevator do?

Answer: ______________

▶ Mechanical Advantage (page 105)

3. Mechanical advantage = $\frac{60\text{ N}}{15\text{ N}}$ = ______________

4. Suppose you exert of force of 2,800 N to lift a desk up onto a porch. But if you use a ramp, you need to exert a force of only 1,400 N to push it up the ramp onto the porch. What is the mechanical advantage of the ramp?

Answer: ______________

▶ Calculating Efficiency (pages 106–107)

5. Efficiency = $\frac{100\text{ J}}{200\text{ J}} \times 100\%$ = ______________

6. You do 4,000 J of work using a sledge hammer. The sledge hammer does 3,000 J of work on the spike. What is the efficiency of the sledge hammer?

Answer: ______________

▶ Advantage of an Inclined Plane (page 111)

7. Ideal mechanical advantage = $\frac{8 \text{ m}}{2 \text{ m}}$ = ______________

8. Suppose you built a ramp to the front door of the post office for people using wheel chairs. The post office door is 3 m above the level of the sidewalk. The ramp you build is 15 m long. What is the ideal mechanical advantage of your ramp?

Answer: ______________________

▶ Advantage of a Lever (page 114)

9. Ideal mechanical advantage = $\frac{4 \text{ m}}{2 \text{ m}}$ = ______________

10. Suppose you held the handles of a wheel barrow 2.4 m from where they are attached to the wheel. The heavy stone in the wheel barrow was 1.2 m from the wheel. What is the ideal mechanical advantage of the wheel barrow?

Answer: ______________________

▶ Advantage of a Wheel and Axle (pages 117–118)

11. Ideal mechanical advantage = $\frac{36 \text{ cm}}{3 \text{ cm}}$ = ______________

12. Suppose the radius of your bicycle's wheel is 30 cm. The radius of the bicycle's axle is just 5 cm. What is the ideal mechanical advantage of that wheel and axle?

Answer: ______________________

Name ______________________ Date __________ Class ______________

CHAPTER 5

ENERGY AND POWER

SECTION 5-1

The Nature of Energy (pages 132–137)

This section explains how work and energy are related. It also identifies the two basic kinds of energy and describes some different forms of energy.

▶ What Is Energy? (pages 132–133)

1. The ability to do work or cause change is called ________________.

2. Why can work be thought of as the transfer of energy? ______________

____

____

▶ Kinetic Energy (pages 133–134)

3. What are the two general kinds of energy?

 a. ________________ b. ________________

4. What is kinetic energy? ______________________________

5. The kinetic energy of an object depends on both its ______________

 and its ______________.

6. Kinetic energy increases as velocity ______________.

7. What formula do you use to calculate kinetic energy?

____

8. Because velocity is squared in the kinetic energy equation, doubling an

 object's velocity will ______________ its kinetic energy.

▶ Potential Energy (pages 134–135)

9. What is potential energy? ____

____

10. What is the potential energy called that is associated with objects that can be stretched or compressed? ______________________

11. What is potential energy called that depends on height? ______________

____

12. What is the formula you use to determine the gravitational potential energy of an object? ______________________

13. Is the following sentence true or false? The greater the height of an object, the greater its gravitational potential energy. ______________

▶ Different Forms of Energy (pages 136–137)

14. What is mechanical energy? ____

____

15. What is thermal energy? ____

____

____

16. Is the following sentence true or false? When the thermal energy of an object increases, its particles move faster. ______________

17. The potential energy stored in chemical bonds that hold chemical compounds together is called ______________________.

18. What kind of energy is stored in the foods you eat? ______________

19. The energy that moving electric charges carry is called ______________ energy.

Name ______________________ Date __________ Class ______________

20. What kind of energy is stored in the nucleus of an atom?

____

21. Complete the table below on the different forms of energy.

Different Forms of Energy	
Form of Energy	**Examples**
Mechanical energy	
Thermal energy	
Chemical energy	
Electrical energy	
Electromagnetic energy	
Nuclear energy	

Reading Skill Practice

Outlining is a way to help yourself understand and remember what you have read. Write an outline of Section 5–1, The Nature of Energy. In your outline, copy the headings in the textbook. Under each heading, write the main idea of that part of the section. Then list the details that support, or back up, the main idea.

SECTION 5–2

Energy Conversion and Conservation

(pages 140–145)

This section explains how different forms of energy are related and describes the law of conservation of energy.

▶ Conversions Between Forms of Energy (page 141)

1. A change from one form of energy to another is called a(n)

______________________.

2. Is the following sentence true or false? Most forms of energy can be converted into other forms. ______________

3. Describe the conversion of chemical energy to mechanical energy in your body. ____

____

____

▶ Kinetic and Potential Energy (pages 142–143)

4. When you throw an orange up into the air, what kind of energy increases as its height increases? ______________

5. As an orange falls from its greatest height, what kind of energy increases and what kind of energy decreases? ______________

____

____

6. On the diagram of a moving pendulum, label the places where the pendulum has maximum potential energy and where it has maximum kinetic energy.

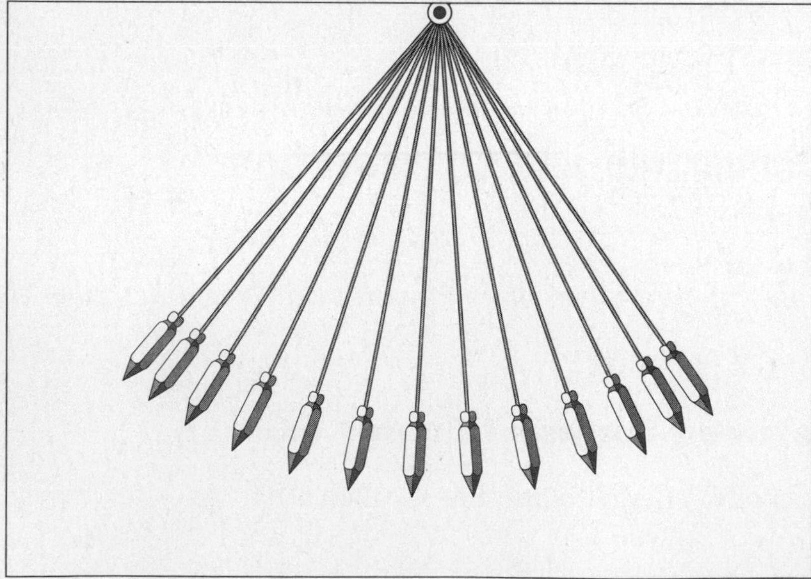

Name ______________________ Date __________ Class ______________

▶ Conservation of Energy (pages 144–145)

7. What does the law of conservation of energy state? ______________________________

____

____

8. Friction converts mechanical energy to ______________ energy.

9. Circle the letter of the sentence that explains why no machine is 100 percent efficient.

   a. Electrical energy is converted to mechanical energy by fuel.

   b. Mechanical energy is converted to thermal energy by friction.

   c. Thermal energy is converted to mechanical energy by friction.

   d. Mechanical energy is converted to electrical energy by a spark.

10. How did Albert Einstein's theory of relativity change the law of conservation of energy? ______________________________

____

____

____

11. Is the following sentence true or false? Matter and energy can be converted back and forth. ______________

▶ Conserving Energy (page 145)

12. Compare and contrast the meanings of *conserving energy* in the table.

	Conserving Energy
In Environmental Science	
In Physical Science	

SECTION 5-3 Energy Conversions and Fossil Fuels
(pages 146–149)

This section explains the source of the energy stored in fossil fuels and describes how energy is converted when fossil fuels are used.

▶ Formation of Fossil Fuels (pages 147–149)

1. Is the following sentence true or false? A fuel is a material that stores chemical potential energy. ______________

2. Circle the letters of the following that are fossil fuels.

a. coal **b.** sunlight **c.** petroleum **d.** natural gas

3. Where did the energy in fossil fuels originally come from?

____

4. What energy conversion takes place on the sun? ______________

____

____

5. What energy conversion takes place during photosynthesis?

____

____

▶ Use of Fossil Fuels (page 149)

6. How is the potential chemical energy of fossil fuels released?

____

7. The process of burning fossil fuels is known as ______________.

8. What energy conversion occurs during combustion? ______________

____

____

9. In a modern coal-fired power plant, the mechanical energy of turbines is converted into electrical energy by ______________.

SECTION 5-4 Power
(pages 150-154)

This section describes how you calculate power and explains the difference between power and energy.

▶ What Is Power? (pages 150–151)

1. What is power? ____

____

____

2. Is the following sentence true or false? You exert more power when you run up a flight of stairs than when you walk up the stairs.

____

3. Circle the letter of each sentence that is true about a device that is twice as powerful as another device.

   a. The more powerful device can do half the amount of work in half the time.

   b. The more powerful device can do the same amount of work in half the time.

   c. The more powerful device can do twice the amount of work in the same amount of time.

   d. The more powerful device can do twice the amount of work in twice the amount of time.

4. What is the formula you use to calculate power?

____

5. Rewrite the equation for power in a way that shows what work equals.

____

CHAPTER 5, Energy and Power *(continued)*

6. 1 J/s = 1 ______________

7. Is the following sentence true or false? Power is often measured in larger units than watts. ______________

8. 1 kilowatt = ______________ watts

9. Is the following sentence true or false? An electric power plant produces millions of kilowatts. ______________

▶ Power and Energy (pages 152–153)

10. Is the following sentence true or false? Power is limited to situations in which objects are moved. ______________

11. Power is the ______________ at which energy is transferred from one object to another or converted from one form to another.

12. The power of a light bulb is the rate at which ______________ energy is converted into ______________ energy and ______________ energy.

13. Why is a 100-watt light bulb brighter than a 40-watt light bulb?

____

____

____

▶ Horsepower (page 154)

14. Circle the letter of each sentence that is true about the unit known as horsepower.
    - **a.** Horsepower is an SI unit of power.
    - **b.** James Watt used the word *horsepower* to compare the work of a steam engine with the work of a horse.
    - **c.** People use the unit horsepower when talking about automobile engines.
    - **d.** 1 horsepower = 746 watts

Name ______________________________ Date __________ Class ________________

WordWise

Complete the following paragraphs using the list of words and phrases below. Each word or phrase is used only once.

Word Bank

law of conservation of energy	nuclear energy	kinetic energy	thermal energy
fossil fuels	electromagnetic energy	energy conversion	electrical energy
power	energy	mechanical energy	potential energy
chemical energy			

In nature, things are constantly changing, and the identification of what causes changes is important in physical science. The ability to do work or cause change is called ________________. There are two general kinds of energy. The energy of motion is called ________________________. Energy that is stored and held in readiness is called ________________________.

There are different forms of the two general kinds of energy. The energy associated with the motion or position of an object is called ________________________. The total energy of the particles of an object is called ________________________. The potential energy stored in chemical bonds that hold chemical compounds together is called ________________________. The energy that moving electric charges carry is called ________________________. Visible light and other waves of energy are forms of ________________________. The energy stored in the nucleus of an atom is ________________________.

Most forms of energy can be converted into other forms. A change from one form of energy to another is called ________________________. Such changes from one form of energy to another do not mean any energy is lost. The ______________________________ states that when one form of energy is converted to another, no energy is destroyed in the process.

A fuel is a material that stores chemical potential energy. For many purposes, we use ________________, such as coal, petroleum, and natural gas. The energy conversions in modern coal-fired power plants result in the electricity you use for home electrical devices. You use these devices to do work. The rate at which work is done, or the amount of work done in a unit of time, is called ________________.

MathWise

For the problems below, show your calculations. If you need more space, use another sheet of paper. Write the answers for the problems on the lines below.

▶ Calculating Gravitational Potential Energy (page 135)

1. Gravitational potential energy = 25 N × 10 m = ________________

2. A student stands at the edge of a diving board that is 3 m high. The student's weight is 350 N. What is the student's gravitational potential energy?

   Answer: ______________________________

3. Gravitational potential energy = 60 kg × 9.8 m/s² × 5 m = __________

4. Suppose a boulder has a mass of 25 kg, and it is perched on the edge of a cliff that is 45 m high. What is the gravitational potential energy of the boulder?

   Answer: ______________________________

▶ Calculating Power (pages 150–151)

5. Power = $\dfrac{5{,}000\ \text{N} \times 15\ \text{m}}{3\ \text{s}}$ = ________________

6. You exert a force of 300 N to lift a box 2 m from the floor to a shelf in 3 s. How much power did you use?

   Answer: ______________________________

Name ______________________ Date __________ Class ______________

CHAPTER 6

THERMAL ENERGY AND HEAT

SECTION 6-1

Temperature and Thermal Energy

(pages 160–162)

This section describes the three common temperature scales and explains how temperature differs from thermal energy.

▶ Temperature (pages 160–161)

1. Is the following sentence true or false? All particles of matter have kinetic energy. ______________

2. What is temperature? ____

____

____

3. Which particles are moving faster, the particles of a mug of hot cocoa or the particles of a glass of cold chocolate milk? ______________

____

____

▶ Temperature Scales (pages 161–162)

4. What are the three common scales for measuring temperature?

   a. ______________ b. ______________ c. ______________

5. The most common temperature scale in the United States is the

   ______________ scale.

6. The temperature scale used in most of the world is the

   ______________ scale.

7. The temperature scale commonly used in physical science is the

   ________________ scale.

8. What are the intervals on the Fahrenheit scale called?

   ____

9. Which scale is divided into 100 equal parts between the freezing and boiling of water? ______________________

10. What is the temperature called at which no more energy can be removed from matter? ______________________

11. Complete the following table. See Figure 2 on page 161.

Temperature Scales			
Scale	**Absolute zero**	**Water freezes**	**Water boils**
Fahrenheit	–460°		
	–273°		100°
	0	273	

▶ Thermal Energy (page 162)

12. The total energy of the particles in a substance is called

    ________________ energy.

13. Circle the letter of each sentence that is true of thermal energy.

    a. Thermal energy partly depends on the temperature of a substance.

    b. Thermal energy partly depends on the scale used to measure the temperature of a substance.

    c. Thermal energy partly depends on how the particles of a substance are arranged.

    d. Thermal energy partly depends on the number of particles of a substance.

Name ______________________ Date __________ Class ______________

SECTION 6–2

The Nature of Heat

(pages 163–169)

This section explains how heat is related to thermal energy and describes three ways heat is transferred.

▶ Introduction (pages 163–164)

1. What is heat? ____

____

____

____

2. Is the following sentence true or false? Heat is thermal energy moving from a warmer object to a cooler object. ____________________

▶ How Is Heat Transferred? (pages 164–166)

3. Circle the letter of the three ways that heat can move.

   a. conduction **b.** current **c.** radiation **d.** convection

4. Think of a metal spoon in a pot of hot water. How do the particles of the water affect the particles of the spoon? ____________________

____

____

____

____

5. How is heat transferred in convection? ______________________

____

____

6. The circular motion of fluid caused by rising and sinking of heated and cooler fluid is known as a(n) ____________________.

7. The illustration shows a pot of liquid on a stovetop burner. Draw the convection currents that result.

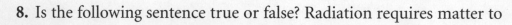

8. Is the following sentence true or false? Radiation requires matter to transfer energy. ______________

9. Complete the table.

Heat Transfer		
Process	**How Heat Moves**	**Example**
Conduction		
Convection		
Radiation		

▶ Heat Moves One Way (page 166)

10. When heat flows from one substance to another, what happens to the temperature of the substance giving off the heat and to the temperature of the substance receiving the heat? ______________________________

____

____

____

11. Why can't ice transfer coldness into another substance? ______________

____

____

▶ Conductors and Insulators (pages 167–168)

12. A material that conducts heat well is called a(n) ______________.

13. A material that does not conduct heat well is called a(n)

______________.

14. Classify each of the following materials as either a conductor or an insulator by writing the correct term on the line.

a. air	______________	b. wool	______________
c. wood	______________	d. tile	______________
e. silver	______________	f. fiberglass	______________

▶ Specific Heat (pages 168–169)

15. What is a substance's specific heat? ______________

____

____

16. What is the unit of measure for specific heat? ______________

____

17. Materials with a high specific heat can absorb a great deal of thermal energy without a great change in ______________.

18. The energy gained or lost by an object is related to which of the following? Circle the letter of the terms that answer the question.

a. mass b. volume c. specific heat d. temperature

19. What is the formula you can use to calculate thermal energy changes?

____

SECTION 6-3

Thermal Energy and States of Matter

(pages 173–178)

This section explains what causes matter to change state. It also explains why matter expands when it is heated.

▶ Three States of Matter (page 174)

1. Is the following sentence true or false? All matter can exist in three states.

   ____

2. Circle the letter of the terms that identify states of matter.

   a. water **b.** gas **c.** liquid **d.** solid

3. The particles that make up a(n) ______________ are packed together in a relatively fixed position.

4. Circle the letter of each statement that is true about liquids.

   a. Liquids have a definite volume.

   b. Liquids have a fixed shape.

   c. Liquid particles can move around.

   d. Liquid particles are moving around so fast that they don't even stay close together.

5. In which state of matter can the particles only vibrate back and forth?

   ____

6. In which state of matter do the particles expand to fill all the space available? ______________

▶ Changes of State (pages 174–175)

7. What is a change of state? ______________________________

   ____

   ____

8. Circle the letter of each sentence that is true.
   a. The particles of a gas move faster than the particles of a liquid.
   b. The particles of a solid move faster than the particles of a gas.
   c. The particles of a liquid move faster than the particles of a solid.
   d. The particles of a gas move faster than the particles of a solid.

9. Matter will change from one state to another if ______________________ is absorbed or released.

10. On the graph below, write labels for the regions of the graph that represent the gas, liquid, and solid states of matter.

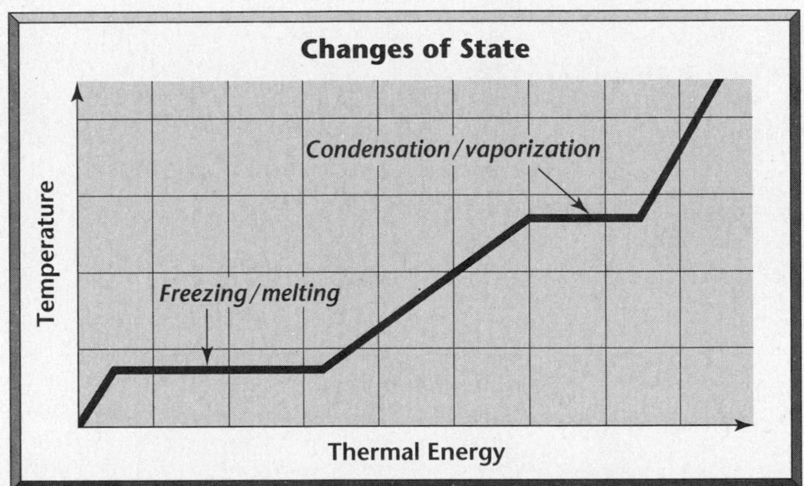

▶ Solid-Liquid Changes of State (pages 175–176)

11. The change in state from a solid to a liquid is called ______________.

12. The temperature at which a solid changes to a liquid is called the ______________________.

13. The change in state from a liquid to a solid is called ______________.

14. The temperature at which a substance changes from a liquid to a solid is called its ______________________.

▶ Liquid-Gas Changes of State (pages 176–177)

15. What is vaporization? ____
____

16. If vaporization takes place on the surface of a liquid it is called

_______________.

17. What is vaporization called when it occurs below the surface of a liquid? _______________

18. The temperature at which liquid boils is called its _______________.

19. A change from the gas state to the liquid state is called

_______________.

▶ Thermal Expansion (pages 177–178)

20. The expanding of matter when it is heated is known as

_______________.

21. What happens to the liquid in a thermometer when it is heated?

____

22. Heat-regulating devices are called _______________.

23. In thermostats, what are strips of two different metals joined together called? _______________

24. In thermostats, bimetallic strips are used because different metals

_______________ at different rates.

Reading Skill Practice

You can often increase your understanding of what you've read by making comparisons. A compare/contrast table helps you do this. On a separate sheet of paper, draw a table to compare the three states of matter as explained on page 174. The three row heads will be *Solid, Liquid,* and *Gas*. Column heads should include *State, Particles, Shape,* and *Volume*. For more information about compare/contrast tables, see page 832 in the Skills Handbook of your textbook.

Name ______________________ Date __________ Class ______________

SECTION 6-4

Uses of Heat

(pages 179–182)

This section describes how thermal energy is related to heat engines and refrigerators.

▶ Heat Engines (pages 179–181)

1. To fire a steam locomotive, the thermal energy of a coal fire must be converted to the ______________ energy of the moving train.

2. The conversion of thermal energy to mechanical energy requires a device called a(n) ______________________.

3. What is the process of burning a fuel, such as coal or gasoline?

   ____

4. How are heat engines classified? ______________________________

   ____

   ____

5. Complete the compare/contrast table.

Heat Engines		
Type	**Where Fuel Is Burned**	**Example**
External combustion engines		
Internal combustion engines		

6. In a steam engine, what does the steam move back and forth inside a cylinder? ______________

7. In an internal combustion engine, each up or down movement of a piston is called a(n) ______________.

8. When a spark ignites the mixture of gas and fuel in a four-stroke engine, stored chemical energy is converted to ______________ energy.

9. Complete the flowchart below, which describes the process that occurs in each cylinder of a four-stroke engine.

A mixture of fuel and air is drawn into the cylinder during the ______________ stroke.

↓

During the ______________ stroke, the mixture is squeezed into a smaller space.

↓

A spark plug ignites the mixture during ______________, heating up the gas.

↓

During the ______________ stroke, the heated gas expands and pushes the piston down, which moves the crankshaft.

↓

During the ______________ stroke, the piston pushes the heated gas out, making room for new fuel and air.

▶ Refrigerators (page 182)

10. A refrigerator transfers thermal energy from a cool area to a(n) ______________ area.

11. What provides the energy for a refrigerator to transfer energy from inside to outside? ______________________________

____

12. Where does the gas that circulates through the tubes inside the refrigerator walls lose thermal energy? ______________________

____

Name ______________________ Date __________ Class ______________

WordWise

Use the clues below to identify key terms from Chapter 6. Write the terms on the lines, putting one letter in each blank. When you finish, the word enclosed in the diagonal will reveal an important term related to kinetic energy.

Clues

1. The expanding of matter when it is heated
2. Thermal energy that is transferred
3. Process of burning a fuel
4. Process by which matter changes from the liquid to the gas state
5. Heat is transferred by the movement of these currents.
6. Vaporization that takes place at the surface of a liquid
7. A material that does not conduct heat well
8. The change of state from solid to liquid
9. The temperature at which no more energy can be removed from matter
10. A material that conducts heat well
11. The physical change from one state of matter to another

1. _ _ _ _ _ _ _   _ _ _ _ _ _ _ _ _
2. _ _ _ _
3. _ _ _ _ _ _ _ _ _ _
4. _ _ _ _ _ _ _ _ _ _ _ _
5. _ _ _ _ _ _ _ _ _ _
6. _ _ _ _ _ _ _ _ _ _ _
7. _ _ _ _ _ _ _ _ _
8. _ _ _ _ _ _ _
9. _ _ _ _ _ _ _ _   _ _ _ _
10. _ _ _ _ _ _ _ _ _
11. _ _ _ _ _ _   _ _   _ _ _ _ _

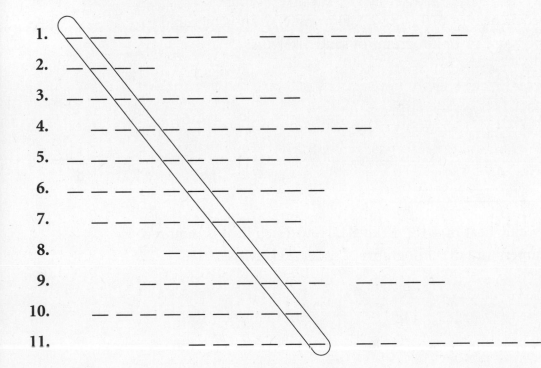

MathWise

For the problems below, show your calculations. If you need more space, use another sheet of paper. Write the answers for the problems on the lines below.

▶ Specific Heat (pages 168–169)

1. Heat absorbed = (2 kg)(450 J/(kg·K))(5 K) = _______________

2. Heat absorbed = (7 kg)(664 J/(kg·K))(20 K) = _______________

3. Aluminum has a specific heat of 903 J/(kg·K). How much heat is required to raise the temperature of 6 kilograms of aluminum 15 kelvins?

   Answer: _______________

4. Sand has a specific heat of 670 J/(kg·K). How much heat is required to raise the temperature of 16 kilograms of sand 5 kelvins?

   Answer: _______________

5. Water has a specific heat of 4,180 J/(kg·K). How much heat is required to raise the temperature of 3 kilograms of water 20 kelvins?

   Answer: _______________

Name ____________________ Date __________ Class ____________

CHAPTER 7

CHARACTERISTICS OF WAVES

SECTION 7-1 What Are Waves? (pages 196–199)

This section explains what causes waves and identifies the three main types of waves.

▶ Waves and Energy (pages 196–197)

1. What is a wave? ____

____

____

2. The material through which a wave travels is called a(n) ______________.

3. Circle the letter of each of the following that can act as mediums.

   a. solids **b.** liquids **c.** gases **d.** empty space

4. Waves that require a medium through which to travel are called

   ____________________.

5. Is the following sentence true or false? When waves travel through a medium, they carry the medium with them. ______________

6. Explain what happens to a duck on the surface of a pond when a wave passes under it. ____

____

7. Give an example of a wave that can travel through empty space. ________

____

8. Waves are created when a source of energy causes a medium to

   ________________.

9. What is a vibration? ____

____

____

▶ Types of Waves (pages 198–199)

10. How are waves classified? ____

____

11. Waves that move the medium at right angles to the direction in which the waves are traveling are called ______________________.

12. Suppose you move the free end of a rope up and down to create a wave. In that case, the rope is the medium. What is the relationship between the movement of the wave and the movement of the particles of the medium?

____

____

13. The highest parts of a transverse wave are called ______________________.

14. The lowest parts of a transverse wave are called ______________________.

15. What type of waves move the particles of the medium parallel to the direction that the waves are traveling? ______________________

16. In longitudinal waves in a spring, the parts where the coils are close together are called ______________________.

17. In longitudinal waves in a spring, the parts where the coils are spread out are called ______________________.

18. Waves that are combinations of transverse and longitudinal waves are called ______________________.

19. Where do surface waves occur? ____

____

Name ______________________ Date __________ Class ______________

20. In surface waves, the combination of motions produces

________________.

21. Complete this concept map about types of waves.

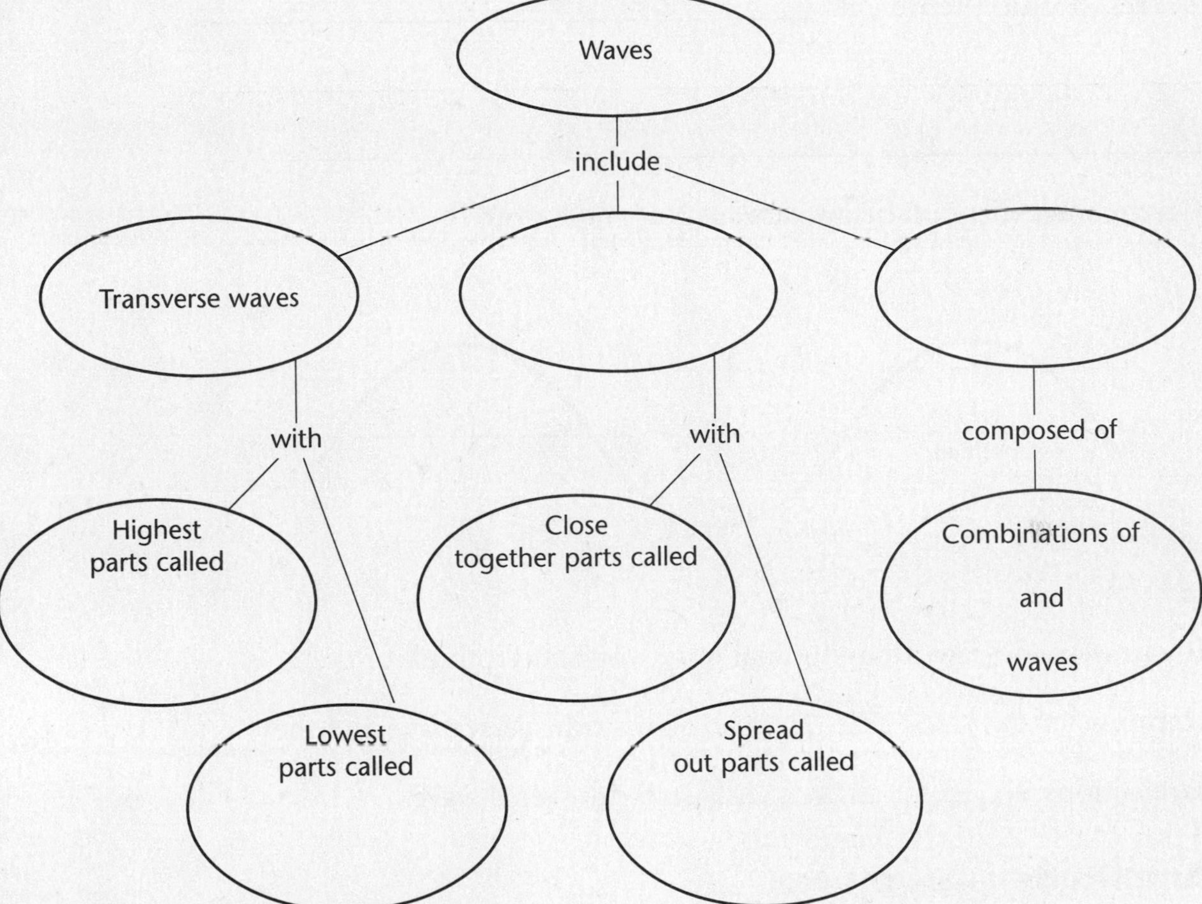

SECTION 7-2 Properties of Waves (pages 200–205)

This section describes the basic properties of waves. It also explains how a wave's speed is related to its wavelength and frequency.

▶ Introduction (page 200)

1. What are the basic properties of waves?

   a. ________________ b. ________________

   c. ________________ d. ________________

▶ Wave Diagrams (pages 200–201)

2. On the transverse wave in Figure 5 on page 201, what does the line called the rest position represent? ______________________________

____

____

3. On the wave diagram below, label a crest and a trough.

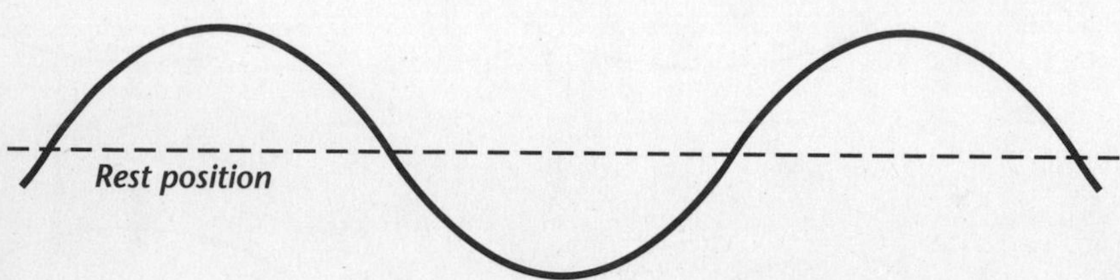

4. If you were to draw a longitudinal wave, you should think of the compressions as ________________ on a transverse wave and the rarefactions as ________________ on a transverse wave.

▶ Amplitude (pages 201–202)

5. The maximum distance the particles of the medium carrying a wave move away from their rest position is called the wave's ________________.

6. Explain what the amplitude of a water wave is. ________________

____

____

7. The amplitude of a wave is a direct measure of its ________________.

8. What is the amplitude of a longitudinal wave? ________________

____

____

9. Circle the letter of each phrase that correctly defines the amplitude of a transverse wave.

   a. The distance from the bottom of a trough to the top of a crest

   b. The maximum distance the particles of the medium move up or down from their rest position

   c. The maximum distance from one point on the rest position to another point on the rest position

   d. The distance from the rest position to a crest or to a trough

10. Suppose a longitudinal wave has crowded compressions and loose rarefactions. Does it have a large or a small amplitude?

____

▶ Wavelength (page 203)

11. The distance between two corresponding parts of a wave is its _______________.

12. How can you find the wavelength of a longitudinal wave? _______________

____

▶ Frequency (page 204)

13. The number of complete waves that pass a given point in a certain amount of time is called the wave's _______________.

14. If you make a wave in a rope so that one wave passes every second, what is its frequency? _______________

15. Circle the letter of the unit used to measure frequency.

   a. watt   b. seconds   c. joule   d. hertz

▶ Speed (pages 204–205)

16. The speed of a wave is how far the wave travels in one unit of _______________.

Complete the following formulas.

17. Speed = ______________________

18. Frequency = ______________________

19. Wavelength = ______________________

20. Circle the letter of each sentence that is true about the speed of waves.

a. All sound waves travel at the same speed.

b. In a given medium and under the same conditions, the speed of a wave is constant.

c. If the temperature and pressure of air changes, the speed of sound waves traveling through the air will change.

d. Waves in different mediums travel at different speeds.

21. If you increase the frequency of a wave, the wavelength must

______________.

SECTION 7-3 Interactions of Waves (pages 206–211)

This section describes how waves bend and how waves interact with each other.

▶ Reflection (page 206)

1. On the illustration below, write labels and draw arrows to show the location of the angle of incidence and the angle of reflection.

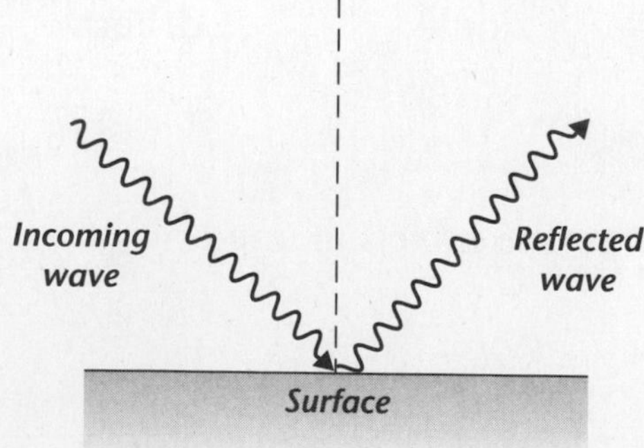

Name ______________________ Date __________ Class __________

2. The bouncing back of a wave when it hits a surface through which it cannot pass is called ______________.

3. What does the law of reflection state? ______________________

____

4. Is the following sentence true or false? Only transverse waves obey the law of reflection. ______________

▶ Refraction (page 207)

5. What happens when a wave moves from one medium into another medium at an angle? ______________________

____

____

6. The bending of waves as they enter a different medium is called ______________.

7. All waves change speed when they enter a new medium, but they don't always bend. When does bending occur? ______________________

____

____

8. The bending of a wave entering a new medium occurs because the two sides of the wave are traveling at different ______________.

▶ Diffraction (pages 207–208)

9. What happens when a wave passes a barrier or moves through a hole in a barrier? ______________________

____

10. The bending of waves around the edge of a barrier is known as ______________.

11. Look at Figure 11 on page 208. What happens when waves go through a hole in a barrier? ______

▶ Interference (pages 208–209)

12. When two waves meet, they have an effect on each other. This interaction is called ______.

13. When does constructive interference occur? ______

14. Describe what Figure 12A on page 209 shows. ______

15. When the amplitudes of two waves combine with each other to produce a smaller amplitude, the result is called ______.

16. In Figure 12B on page 209, why does the resulting wave at the bottom have an amplitude of zero? ______

17. What happens when two identical waves travel along the same path, one a little behind the other? ______

Name ______________________ Date __________ Class __________

▶ Standing Waves (pages 209–211)

18. What is a standing wave? ______________________

____

____

19. When destructive interference causes two waves to combine to produce an amplitude of zero, the point is called a(n) ______________.

20. The crests and troughs of a standing wave are called ______________.

21. Is the following sentence true or false? Most objects have a natural frequency of vibration. ______________

22. When does resonance occur? ______________________

____

____

23. Why are marching troops told to break step as they cross a bridge?

____

____

____

Match the interaction of water waves with its description.

Interaction	Description
_____ **24.** refraction	**a.** When two waves combine to make a wave with a smaller amplitude
_____ **25.** diffraction	**b.** When a wave bends as it moves from deep water to shallow water
_____ **26.** constructive interference	**c.** When two waves combine to make a wave with a larger amplitude
_____ **27.** destructive interference	**d.** When a wave bounces back from a barrier at the same angle it hits
_____ **28.** reflection	**e.** When waves bend or spread out around or behind an obstacle

Reading Skill Practice

You may sometimes forget the meanings of key terms that were introduced earlier in the textbook. When this happens, you can check the meanings of the terms in the Glossary, on pages 848–859, which gives meanings of all the key terms in the textbook. You'll find the terms in alphabetical order. Use the Glossary to review the meanings of all the key terms introduced in Section 7–3. Write their definitions on a separate sheet of paper.

SECTION 7–4 Seismic Waves

(pages 214–216)

This section explains how earthquakes produce waves that move through Earth.

▶ Types of Seismic Waves (page 215)

1. What movement creates stress on rock beneath Earth's surface? ________

____

____

2. What happens when stress on rock builds up enough? ________________

____

____

3. The waves produced by earthquakes are known as

____________________.

4. Circle the letter of each sentence that is true about seismic waves.

   a. Seismic waves can travel from one side of Earth to the other.

   b. Even though seismic waves move through Earth, they don't carry energy.

   c. There is only one kind of seismic wave.

   d. Seismic waves ripple out in all directions from the point where the earthquake occurred.

5. Why can't secondary waves travel through Earth's core? ______________

____

____

6. Which type of seismic waves arrives at distant points before any other seismic waves? ______________

7. Which type of seismic waves produces the most severe ground movements? ______________

8. Which type of seismic waves cannot be detected on the side of Earth opposite an earthquake? ______________

9. What are tsunamis? ______________________________

____

____

10. Complete the table about seismic waves.

Seismic Waves		
Type of Seismic Wave	**Transverse or Longitudinal?**	**Travel Characteristics**
		Travel through all parts of Earth
Secondary waves		Travel through Earth but not through ________
		Travel only along Earth's ________

▶ Detecting Seismic Waves (page 216)

11. Circle the letter of the instrument scientists use to detect earthquakes.

a. rarefactions **b.** telegraphs **c.** seismographs **d.** tsunamis

12. What does a seismograph record? ______________________

____

____

13. What is the frame of a seismograph attached to? ______________________

____

14. What happens to a seismograph's frame when seismic waves arrive?

____

15. How can scientists tell how far away an earthquake was from a seismograph? ______________________

____

16. How can scientists tell where an earthquake occurred? ______________

____

____

17. Complete the flowchart about how geologists locate valuable substances under Earth's surface.

To find out what is underground, geologists set off ______________.

↓

The explosives produce a small ______________.

↓

The small earthquake sends out ______________.

↓

The seismic waves reflect from structures deep ______________.

↓

The reflected seismic waves are recorded by ______________ located around the site of the explosion.

Name ______________________ Date __________ Class ______________

WordWise

The block of letters below contains 16 key terms from Chapter 7. You might find them across, down, or on the diagonal. Use the clues to identify the terms you need to find. Circle each of the terms in the block of letters.

Clues

1. A disturbance that transfers energy from place to place
2. The ability to do work
3. The material through which a wave travels
4. A repeated back-and-forth or up-and-down motion
5. The highest part of a wave
6. The lowest part of a wave
7. The maximum distance the particles of the medium carrying the wave move away from their rest position
8. The distance between two corresponding parts of a wave
9. The number of complete waves that pass a given point in a certain amount of time
10. The unit in which frequency is measured
11. The bending of waves due to a change of speed
12. The bending of waves around the edge of a barrier
13. A point of zero amplitude on a standing wave
14. A point of maximum amplitude on a standing wave
15. What occurs when vibrations traveling through an object match the object's natural frequency
16. A huge surface wave on the ocean caused by an earthquake

d t s u n a m i p a q w
i v i b r a t i o n m a
f r e q u e n c y t a v
f u n n p w b v x i m e
r e f r a c t i o n p l
a x e n e r g y u o l e
c i w a v e z a p d i n
t z e e v s z u j e t g
i o d d e t x w e g u t
o o u t r o u g h y d h
n i r e s o n a n c e r
n y h m e d i u m r t z

MathWise

For the problems below, show your calculations. If you need more space, use another sheet of paper. Write the answers for the problems on the lines below.

▶ Calculating Speed, Frequency, and Wavelength (pages 204–205)

1. Speed = 25 cm × 4 Hz = ____________

2. A wave has a wavelength of 18 mm and a frequency of 3 Hz. At what speed does the wave travel?

   Answer: ____________

3. Frequency = $\frac{75 \text{ cm/s}}{5 \text{ cm}}$ = ____________

4. The speed of a wave is 16 m/s and its wavelength is 4 m. What is its frequency?

   Answer: ____________

5. Wavelength = $\frac{60 \text{ cm/s}}{3 \text{ Hz}}$ = ____________

6. The speed of a wave on a violin is 125 m/s, and the frequency is 1,000 Hz. What is the wavelength of the wave?

   Answer: ____________

Name ______________________ Date __________ Class ______________

CHAPTER 8

SOUND

SECTION 8-1 The Nature of Sound
(pages 222-226)

This section explains what sound is and identifies the factors that affect the speed of sound.

▶ Sound and Longitudinal Waves (pages 222–224)

1. What is sound? ____

____

2. Suppose a sound is made far away from you. When do you hear the sound?

____

____

3. Complete the flowchart about how you make sound with your voice.

You force air through the vocal cords of your ________________.

↓

The air rushing past your vocal cords makes them ________________.

↓

The vibrating vocal cords produce longitudinal waves in the ________________.

↓

The longitudinal waves in the air travel to yours and others' ________________.

4. Why doesn't sound travel through outer space? ____________________

____

____

____

5. What happens to sound waves when they go through a doorway into a room? ____________________

____

▶ The Speed of Sound (pages 224–225)

6. The speed of a sound depends on these three properties of the medium.

a. ____________ **b.** ____________ **c.** ____________

7. Use the table in Figure 4 on page 224 to answer the following question. Through which medium does sound travel faster, air or water?

____

8. The ability of a material to bounce back after being disturbed is called ____________.

9. Is the following sentence true or false? Sound travels more slowly in mediums that have a high degree of elasticity. ____________

10. How much matter, or mass, there is in a given amount of space, or volume, is called ____________.

11. Is the following sentence true or false? In materials in the same state of matter, sound travels slower in denser mediums. ____________

12. Why does sound travel slower through a medium when it is at a low temperature? ____________________

____

▶ Moving Faster Than Sound (page 226)

13. In 1947, what did Captain Chuck Yeager do that nobody had ever done before? ______________________________

____

14. In 1997, what did Andy Green do that nobody had ever done before?

____

____

SECTION 8-2 Properties of Sound
(pages 228–233)

This section describes several properties of sound, including loudness and pitch. It also explains what you hear as the source of a sound moves.

▶ Intensity and Loudness (pages 228–229)

1. The amount of energy a wave carries per second through a unit area is called the sound wave's ______________.

2. Describe the molecules of the medium when a sound wave carries a large amount of energy. ______________________________

____

3. What is loudness? ______________________________

____

4. In what units is loudness measured? ______________

5. Each 10 dB increase in sound level represents how much of an increase in intensity? ______________

6. Can loud music cause damage to your ears? ______________

____

▶ Frequency and Pitch (pages 230–231)

7. Circle the letter of each sentence that is true about how a person changes the pitch of sounds when singing.
   a. A person relaxes the vocal cords to produce lower-frequency sound waves.
   b. A person stretches the vocal cords to produce lower-frequency sound waves.
   c. A person stretches the vocal cords to produce higher-frequency sound waves.
   d. A person relaxes the vocal cords to produce higher-frequency sound waves.

8. Sound waves with frequencies above the normal human range of hearing are called ________________.

9. Sound waves with frequencies below the normal human range of hearing are called ________________.

10. What is the pitch of a sound? ______________________________

____

____

11. What does the pitch of a sound you hear depend on? ____________

____

▶ The Doppler Effect (pages 232–233)

12. What is the Doppler effect? ______________________________

____

____

13. Is the following sentence true or false? A sonic boom is a sound shock wave produced when the sound barrier is broken. ________________

Name ______________________ Date __________ Class ______________

14. Complete the table about the Doppler effect.

Doppler Effect		
Action	**Change in Frequency—Higher or Lower?**	**Change in Pitch—Higher or Lower?**
A police car with siren on moves toward you		
A train with a band playing moves away from you		
A train with a band playing moves toward you		
A police car with siren on moves away from you		

SECTION 8-3 Combining Sound Waves (pages 234–241)

This section explains what produces the quality of sounds. It also explains the difference between music and noise and describes what happens when sound waves interact.

▶ Sound Quality (page 235)

1. The resonant frequency of an object produces a pitch called the

   ______________________.

2. When a string vibrates at several frequencies at the same time, the higher frequencies produce sounds called ______________.

3. What describes the quality of the sound you hear? ______________

4. What makes up the timbre of a particular sound? ______________

   ____

   ____

▶ Making Music (pages 236–239)

5. What is music? ______________________________

   ____

   ____

6. How do musicians vary the pitch on stringed instruments? ____________

____

____

7. Why do many stringed instruments have a box? ____________________

____

____

8. What vibrates within a brass instrument that the player can adjust?

____

____

9. What vibrates when a player blows into the mouthpiece of a woodwind instrument? ______________________________________

____

10. Is the following sentence true or false? The sound a percussion instrument makes depends on the material from which it is made.

____

11. Complete the table by classifying each instrument into one of the major groups of instruments—Strings, Brass, Woodwinds, or Percussion.

Musical Instruments			
Instrument	**Major Group**	**Instrument**	**Major Group**
Guitar		Cello	
Drums		Oboe	
Violin		Trumpet	
Trombone		Double bass	
Clarinet		Harp	

▶ Noise (page 237)

12. A mixture of sound waves that do not sound pleasing together is called

_______________.

13. Circle the letter of each sentence that is true about noise.

    a. Sounds that are music to some people are noise to others.

    b. Noise has no pleasing timbre.

    c. Sounds that have rhythm are always called noise.

    d. Noise has no identifiable pitch.

14. The sound produced when notes that have no musical relationship are played together is called _______________.

▶ Interference of Sound Waves (pages 240–241)

15. When does interference of sound waves occur? _______________

____

____

16. Is the following sentence true or false? When the interference of two sound waves is constructive, the sound is louder than either of the two original sounds. _______________

17. The study and description of how well sound can be heard in a particular room or hall is called _______________.

18. Circle the letter of the term that describes the repeated changes in loudness that occurs when sound waves interfere both constructively and destructively.

    a. frequency   b. beats   c. tuners   d. intervals

19. What does a piano tuner do when he or she hears beats? _______________

____

____

Reading Skill Practice

You can often increase your understanding of what you've read by making comparisons. A compare/contrast table helps you to do this. On a separate sheet of paper, draw a table to compare the different instruments in *Exploring Making Music* on pages 238–239. List the five instruments to be compared across the top of your table. Then list the characteristics that will form the basis of your comparison in the left-hand column. These characteristics should include *Major Group, How Music Is Produced,* and *How Pitch Is Changed.* For more information about compare/contrast tables, see page 832 in the Skills Handbook of your textbook.

SECTION 8-4 How You Hear Sound (pages 244-246)

This section describes how you hear sound and explains what causes hearing loss.

▶ How You Hear Sound (pages 244–245)

Match the three main sections of the ear with their functions.

Main Section	Function
______ 1. outer ear	a. Transmits sound waves inward
______ 2. middle ear	b. Funnels sound waves
______ 3. inner ear	c. Converts sound waves into a form the brain can understand

4. The outermost part of your ear collects sound waves and directs them into a narrower region known as the ______________________.

5. What is the eardrum and where is it located? ______________________

____

____

6. What cavity of the inner ear is filled with fluid? ______________

Name ______________________ Date __________ Class ______________

7. What part of the ear contains the three smallest bones in your body?

____

▶ Hearing Loss (page 246)

8. Circle the letter of each cause of hearing loss.

   a. aging   b. injury   c. nerve fibers   d. infection

9. Why is it dangerous to put objects into your ear, even to clean it?

____

____

10. How can a viral or bacterial infection cause hearing loss? __________

____

11. What is the most common type of hearing loss? ______________

____

____

12. When you know you are going to be exposed to loud noises, what should you do to prevent hearing loss? ______________________

____

13. Is the following sentence true or false? Hearing aids are amplifiers.

____

SECTION 8-5 Applications of Sound (pages 248-252)

This section explains how sound waves are used to tell distances. It also describes how animals use sounds and how sound is used in medicine.

▶ Reflection of Sound Waves (page 248)

1. A reflected sound wave is called a(n) ______________.

2. What does a sound wave do when it hits a surface through which it cannot pass? ______________________________

____

▶ Sonar (page 249)

3. Circle the letter of the following that are uses of reflected sound waves.
   a. To raise a sunken ship to the surface of water
   b. To determine the depth of water
   c. To locate boats out on the ocean
   d. To find schools of fish

4. What is sonar? ______________________________

____

5. Complete the flowchart about how sonar works in calculating the depth of the ocean.

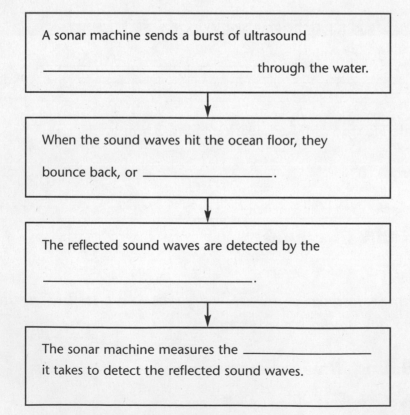

A sonar machine sends a burst of ultrasound ______________________ through the water.

↓

When the sound waves hit the ocean floor, they bounce back, or ______________.

↓

The reflected sound waves are detected by the ______________________.

↓

The sonar machine measures the ______________ it takes to detect the reflected sound waves.

6. What does the intensity of the reflected sound waves tell the sonar machine about the object that reflected the waves? ______

▶ Uses of Ultrasound and Infrasound (pages 250–252)

7. Is the following sentence true or false? Some animals communicate using sounds with frequencies that humans cannot hear.

______

8. The use of sound waves to determine distances or to locate objects is called ______.

9. Describe how a bat uses echolocation to avoid bumping into an object as it flies. ______

10. A picture of the inside of the human body using ultrasound is called a(n) ______.

11. In Figure 25 on page 251, what is the doctor trying to see with the ultrasound machine? ______

12. What are three examples of common household objects that use ultrasound waves? ______

WordWise

Use the clues to help you unscramble the key terms from Chapter 8. Then put the numbered letters in order to find the answer to the riddle.

Clues	Key Terms	
The membrane that separates the outer ear from the middle ear	mrrudae	_ _ _ _ _ _ _ _ (1)
The cavity filled with liquid in the inner ear	ccleoah	_ _ _ _ _ _ _ (2)
How high or low a sound seems to a person	hctip	_ _ _ _ _ (3)
Sound waves with frequencies above the normal human range of hearing	dnuosartlu	_ _ _ _ _ _ _ _ _ _ (4)
The ability of a material to bounce back after being disturbed	ttiiscyale	_ _ _ _ _ _ _ _ _ _ (5)
A mixture of sound waves that do not sound pleasing together	ensoi	_ _ _ _ _ (6)
How well sounds can be heard in a particular room or hall	ccuossiat	_ _ _ _ _ _ _ _ _ (7)
Your voice box	xyarnl	_ _ _ _ _ _ (8)
The quality of the sound you hear	erbmit	_ _ _ _ _ _ (9)
Sound with a pleasing timbre and clear pitch	smcui	_ _ _ _ _ (10)
The sound produced when tones are played together that seem to have no musical relationship	sseaionncd	_ _ _ _ _ _ _ _ _ _ (11)
The amount of energy a sound wave carries per second through a unit area	ynittiens	_ _ _ _ _ _ _ _ _ (12)

Riddle: What is the use of sound to find distance?

Answer: _ _ _ _ _ _ _ _ _ _ _ _
1 2 3 4 5 6 7 8 9 10 11 12

Name ______________________ Date __________ Class ______________

CHAPTER 9

THE ELECTROMAGNETIC SPECTRUM

SECTION 9-1 The Nature of Electromagnetic Waves
(pages 258–261)

This section explains what light is and describes how scientists explain properties of light.

▶ Electromagnetic Waves (pages 259–260)

1. What are electromagnetic waves? ______________________

____

____

2. Is the following sentence true or false? Electromagnetic waves can transfer energy only through a medium. ______________

3. What do electromagnetic waves consist of? ______________________

____

____

4. Complete the table about electric and magnetic fields.

Electric and Magnetic Fields	
Field	**Definition**
Electric field	A region in which
Magnetic field	A region in which

5. The energy that is transferred by electromagnetic waves is called

______________________.

6. Circle the letter of each sentence that is true about electric and magnetic fields.
   a. An electromagnetic wave occurs when electric and magnetic fields vibrate at right angles to each other.
   b. A magnetic field is surrounded by an electric current.
   c. When an electric field vibrates, so does the magnetic field.
   d. An electric current is surrounded by a magnetic field.

7. Is the following sentence true or false? All electromagnetic waves travel at the same speed. ______________

▶ Waves or Particles? (pages 260–261)

8. Light has many of the properties of waves. But light can also act as though it is a stream of ______________.

9. What happens when light enters a polarizing filter? ______________
____

10. The light that passes through a polarizing filter is called ______________.

11. When light passes through a polarizing filter, does it have the properties of a wave or a particle? ______________

12. Is the following sentence true or false? If two polarizing filters are placed so that one is rotated 90° from the other, all light can come through. ______________

13. The movement of electrons in a substance when light is shined on it is called the ______________.

14. The photoelectric effect can only be explained by thinking of light as a stream of tiny packets of energy, or as ______________.

15. What are particles of light energy called? ______________

Name ______________________ Date __________ Class ______________

SECTION 9-2

Waves of the Electromagnetic Spectrum

(pages 262-270)

This section explains how electromagnetic waves differ from one another. It also describes the different waves of the electromagnetic spectrum.

▶ Characteristics of Electromagnetic Waves (pages 262-263)

1. Circle the letter of each sentence that is true about electromagnetic waves.

a. Different electromagnetic waves have different frequencies.

b. All electromagnetic waves have the same wavelength.

c. Different electromagnetic waves have different wavelengths.

d. All electromagnetic waves travel at the same speed.

2. Circle the letter of each sentence that is true about electromagnetic waves.

a. As the wavelength of electromagnetic waves decreases, the frequency increases.

b. Waves with the longest wavelengths have the lowest frequencies.

c. As the frequency of electromagnetic waves decreases, the wavelength increases.

d. Waves with the shortest wavelengths have the lowest frequencies.

3. What is the name for the range of electromagnetic waves when they are placed in order of increasing frequency? ______________________

____

4. Label the electromagnetic spectrum below with the names of the different waves that make up the spectrum.

Electromagnetic Spectrum

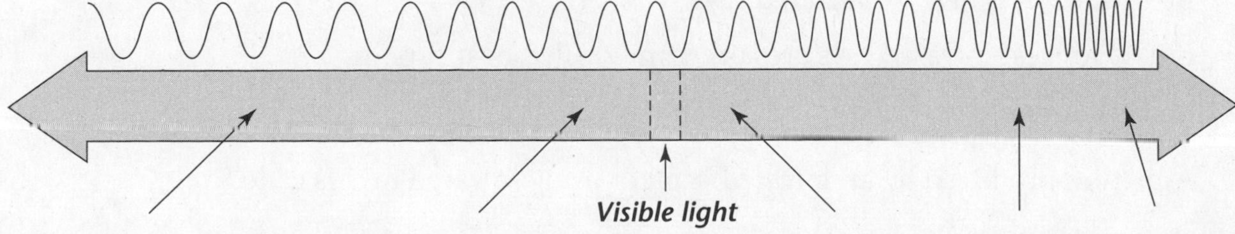

▶ Radio Waves (pages 263–265)

5. Each radio station in an area broadcasts at a different ________________.

6. What does a radio convert radio waves into? ________________

7. Is the following sentence true or false? Microwaves are a kind of radio waves. ________________

8. Circle the letter of the reason why you shouldn't put a metal object in a microwave oven.

a. Microwaves can pass right through metal objects.

b. Microwaves are easily blocked by buildings.

c. Microwaves cause a buildup of electrical energy in metal.

d. Microwaves are easily absorbed into metal objects.

9. A system of detecting reflected microwaves to locate objects is called ________________.

10. What is the use of radio waves in medicine to produce pictures of tissues in the human body called? ________________________________

____

▶ Infrared Rays (pages 265–267)

11. The energy you feel as heat from an electric burner is electromagnetic waves called ________________________.

12. Circle the letter of each sentence that is true about infrared rays.

a. Infrared rays have longer wavelengths than visible light.

b. Most objects give off infrared rays.

c. The longest infrared rays are sometimes called heat rays.

d. Heat lamps give off no infrared rays.

13. A picture produced by an infrared camera using infrared rays is called a(n) ________________.

Name ______________________ Date __________ Class __________

▶ Visible Light (page 268)

14. The part of the electromagnetic spectrum that you can see is called

______________________.

15. Look at Figure 5 on page 263. What are the colors of light that make up visible light? Write their names from longest wavelength to shortest wavelength.

a. ______________ **b.** ______________ **c.** ______________

d. ______________ **e.** ______________ **f.** ______________

16. Is the following sentence true or false? Most visible light is made up of a mixture of the colors in the visible spectrum. ______________

▶ Ultraviolet Rays (pages 268–269)

17. Electromagnetic waves with wavelengths just shorter than those of visible light are called ______________________.

18. Circle the letter of each sentence that is true about ultraviolet rays.

a. Too much exposure to UV rays can cause skin cancer.

b. Humans with good vision can see UV rays.

c. UV rays cause skin cells to produce vitamin D.

d. Lamps that produce UV rays are used to kill bacteria.

▶ X-Rays (page 269)

19. Electromagnetic waves with frequencies higher than ultraviolet rays but lower than gamma rays are ______________________.

20. Circle the letter of the reason why bones show up as lighter areas on photographic plates in an X-ray machine.

a. Bones absorb X-rays and don't allow them to pass through.

b. X-rays pass right through skin and bones.

c. Bones cause the photographic plate in an X-ray machine to darken.

d. X-rays cannot pass through the skin above the photographic plates.

▶ Gamma Rays (page 270)

21. The electromagnetic waves with the shortest wavelengths and the highest frequencies are called ______________________.

22. Why are gamma rays the most penetrating of all the electromagnetic rays?

____

____

SECTION 9-3 Producing Visible Light (pages 272–275)

This section describes different kinds of light bulbs. It also identifies the colors of light produced by the most common kind of light bulb.

▶ Introduction (page 272)

1. Complete the table below by writing the correct term.

Kinds of Objects	
Kind of Object	**Description**
object	An object that can be seen because it reflects light
object	An object that gives off its own light

2. To view the different colors of light produced by each type of light bulb, you can use an instrument called a(n) ________________.

▶ Incandescent Lights (pages 272–273)

3. A light that glows when a filament inside it gets hot is called a(n) ______________________.

4. What is the filament inside a light bulb? ______________________

____

5. Circle the letter of each sentence that is true about incandescent lights.
   - **a.** Most of the energy produced by incandescent bulbs is given off as infrared rays.
   - **b.** Incandescent bulbs give off all the colors of visible light.
   - **c.** Incandescent bulbs are very efficient in giving off light.
   - **d.** Inventor Thomas Edison developed a long-lasting incandescent bulb.

6. Is the following sentence true or false? Less than ten percent of the energy used to operate an incandescent bulb is given out as light.

   ____

▶ Fluorescent Lights (page 273)

7. Lights that glow when an electric current causes ultraviolet waves to strike a coating inside a tube are called ______________________.

8. The process of ultraviolet waves hitting the powder coating inside a fluorescent bulb and causing the coating to emit visible light is called

   ______________.

9. Circle the letter of each sentence that is true about fluorescent lights.
   - **a.** Fluorescent lights give off most of their energy as light.
   - **b.** Each glass fluorescent-light tube contains a gas.
   - **c.** Fluorescent lights emit visible light when UV rays strike the powder coating on the inside of the glass tube.
   - **d.** Fluorescent lights usually don't last as long as incandescent lights.

▶ Neon Lights (page 274)

10. A sealed glass tube filled with neon gas that produces light is called a(n)

    ______________.

11. Circle the letter of each sentence that is true about neon lights.
    - **a.** Neon lights are commonly used for bright, flashy signs.
    - **b.** Pure neon gives out red light.
    - **c.** Each glass neon-light tube is coated on the inside with a powder.
    - **d.** Often, what is called a neon light has a mixture of gases in the tube.

Name ______________________ Date __________ Class ______________

▶ Sodium Vapor Lights (page 274)

12. Circle the letter of each sentence that is true about sodium vapor lights.
    a. Sodium vapor lights require very little electricity for a lot of light.
    b. In a sodium vapor light, heat from gases change sodium from a solid to a gas.
    c. Particles of sodium vapor give off a greenish blue light.
    d. Sodium vapor lights are often used for street lighting.

▶ Tungsten-Halogen Lights (page 275)

13. Circle the letter of each sentence that is true about tungsten-halogen lights.
    a. Tungsten-halogen lights work like fluorescent lights.
    b. The halogen gas in a tungsten-halogen light makes the filament give off a bright white light.
    c. In a tungsten-halogen light, a filament gets hot and glows.
    d. Halogen bulbs become very hot.

▶ Bioluminescence (page 275)

14. The process by which living organisms produce their own light with a chemical reaction is called ______________________.

15. What are three kinds of organisms that produce light through bioluminescence? ______________________

Reading Skill Practice

A flowchart can help you remember the order in which events occur. Create a flowchart that describes how an electric current produces light in an incandescent light, as explained on pages 272–273 of your book. Create a second flowchart that describes how an electric current produces light in a fluorescent light, as explained on page 273 of your book. For more information on flowcharts, see page 833 in the Skills Handbook of your book. Do your work on a separate sheet of paper.

Name ____________________ Date __________ Class __________

SECTION 9-4

Wireless Communication

(pages 278–285)

This section describes how radio waves are used in communication, how cellular phones and pagers work, and how satellites relay information.

▶ Radio and Television (pages 278–281)

1. Is the following sentence true or false? Both radio and television programs are transmitted by radio waves. ____________

2. Look at the radio dial shown in Figure 21 on page 279. What does each number on the dial represent? ____________________

3. Rank the measurements below from highest to lowest frequency. Rank the highest as *1*.

_____ **a.** 1,030 kHz _____ **b.** 107 MHz

_____ **c.** 550 kHz _____ **d.** 95 MHz

4. What does AM stand for? ____________________

5. Complete the flowchart below about the broadcast of AM radio.

The radio station converts sound into ____________________.

↓

These signals are converted into a pattern of changes in the ____________ of radio waves.

↓

The radio station broadcasts the radio waves through the ____________.

↓

Your radio picks up the radio waves and converts them back into ____________________.

6. What does FM stand for? ______________________

7. How do FM signals travel? ______________________

____

____

8. Is the following sentence true or false? The frequencies of FM stations are much lower than the frequencies of AM stations. ______________

9. Why can't FM waves travel as far as AM waves? ______________

____

____

____

10. How are television broadcasts different than radio broadcasts?

____

____

11. What are the two main bands of television wave frequencies?

a. ______________ b. ______________

▶ Cellular Telephones (page 281)

12. Circle the letter of the kind of radio waves that transmit signals from cellular telephones.

a. X-rays b. infrared rays c. gamma rays d. microwaves

13. In a cellular telephone system, what does each cell have? ______________

____

▶ Cordless Telephones (page 282)

14. What kind of waves transmits the signals from the handset to the base of a cordless telephone? ______________

Name ______________________ Date __________ Class ______________

▶ Pagers (pages 282–283)

15. When you leave a message for a pager, how does the information get to the correct pager? ______________________________

____

____

▶ Communications Satellites (pages 284–285)

16. Is the following sentence true or false? Communications satellites arc remote-controlled spacecraft that orbit Earth. ______________

17. Circle the letter of each sentence that is true about communications satellites.
    - **a.** It is necessary to have more than one satellite in orbit for any given purpose.
    - **b.** Communications satellites receive sound waves from Earth and send radio waves back to Earth.
    - **c.** Most satellites strengthen the signals they receive before they send them back to Earth.
    - **d.** Communications satellites can relay several signals at once.

18. How do satellite telephone systems affect long-distance telephone calls?

____

____

19. What do television networks use communications satellites for?

____

____

20. If you had a GPS receiver, what could you determine by receiving signals from the Global Positioning System? ______________

____

____

Name ______________________ Date __________ Class ____________

WordWise

Complete the sentences by using one of the scrambled words below.

Word Bank

ouuilmns	mmargoerht	uoeescntrfl ghtsli	noothp	tionaidar
oidar sevaw	yasr-X	cancentdesin ghtsil	andetimluli	
iielbsv tighl	maggnii	eaoimcrwvs		

The energy that is transferred by electromagnetic waves is called electromagnetic

__________________.

Each tiny packet of light energy is called a(n) __________________.

The radio waves with the longest wavelengths and lowest frequencies are called

__________________________.

The radio waves with the shortest wavelengths and the highest frequencies are

__________________.

The process of using radio waves to produce pictures of tissues in the human body is called magnetic resonance __________________.

A picture taken with an infrared camera that shows regions of different temperatures in different colors is a(n) __________________.

The part of the electromagnetic spectrum that you can see is called __________________.

Electromagnetic waves with wavelengths just a little higher than ultraviolet rays are called __________________.

An object that can be seen because it reflects light is said to be __________________.

An object that gives off its own light is said to be __________________.

Lights that glow when a filament inside them gets hot are called __________________.

Lights that glow when an electric current causes ultraviolet waves to strike a coating inside a tube are called __________________________.

Name ______________________ Date ____________ Class ______________

CHAPTER 10

LIGHT

SECTION 10-1 Reflection and Mirrors
(pages 294–298)

This section describes what happens when light strikes an object and identifies three kinds of mirrors.

▶ When Light Strikes an Object (page 294)

1. What three things can occur when light strikes an object? ______________________

____

____

2. Complete the table about kinds of objects.

Kinds of Objects		
Object	**Description**	**Examples**
	A material that transmits light	
	A material that scatters light as it passes through	
	A material that reflects or absorbs all of the light that strikes it	

▶ Kinds of Reflection (page 295)

3. To show how light travels and reflects, you can represent light waves as straight lines called ______________.

CHAPTER 10, Light *(continued)*

4. What occurs when parallel rays of light hit a smooth surface? __________

____

5. What occurs when parallel rays of light hit a bumpy, or uneven, surface?

____

____

▶ Mirrors (pages 296–298)

6. What is a mirror? ______________________

____

____

7. A copy of an object formed by reflected or refracted rays of light is a(n) ______________.

8. What size of image does a plane mirror produce? ______________

9. An upright image formed where rays of light appear to meet behind a mirror is called a(n) ______________________.

10. The point at which light rays meet is called the ______________.

11. An image formed when rays actually meet at a point is called a(n) ______________________.

12. Complete the table about kinds of mirrors.

Kinds of Mirrors			
Kind of Mirror	**Description**	**Virtual or Real Image?**	**Upright or Inverted?**
	Flat		
	Curved inward	Virtual or real	Inverted or upright
	Curved outward		Upright

Name ______________________ Date __________ Class ______________

SECTION 10-2

Refraction and Lenses

(pages 299–303)

This section explains what happens when light rays enter a medium at an angle. It also describes how images are formed when light is refracted by transparent material.

▶ Refraction of Light (pages 299–301)

1. When light rays enter a new medium at an angle, what does the change in speed cause the rays to do? ______________________

____

____

2. Rank the following mediums according to how fast light travels through them. Rank the fastest as *1*.

_____ **a.** water _____ **b.** glass _____ **c.** air

3. What is a material's index of refraction? ______________________

____

____

4. Glass causes light to bend more than air does. Which material has a higher index of refraction? ______________

5. What does Figure 9 on page 300 show happens to white light when it enters a prism? ______________________

____

____

6. Explain why a rainbow can form when light shines through tiny raindrops of water. ______________________

____

____

7. An image of a distant object caused by the refraction of light is called a(n) ________________.

▶ Lenses (pages 302–303)

8. A curved piece of glass or other transparent material that is used to refract light is called a(n) ________________.

9. How does a lens form an image? ______________________________

____

____

10. Label each lens as either a convex lens or a concave lens. Then show what happens to the light rays as they pass through each lens.

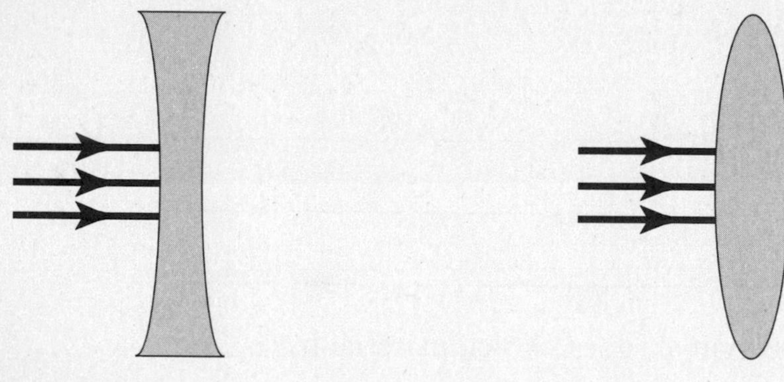

________________ ________________

11. Complete the following table about lenses.

Kinds of Lenses		
Shape of Lens	**Description**	**Image Formed—Real or Virtual?**
	Thinner in the center than at the edges	
Convex		Real or virtual

Name ______________________ Date __________ Class ______________

SECTION 10-3

Color

(pages 305–309)

This section explains what determines the color of an object. It also identifies the primary colors of light and explains how mixing colored substances is different from mixing light.

▶ The Color of Objects (pages 305–307)

1. The color of an object is the color of the light it ______________.

2. Complete the flowchart about why you see the petals of a lily as orange.

______________ light strikes the petals of a lily.

↓

The petals reflect mostly the ______________________.

↓

The petals absorb the ______________________ of light other than orange.

↓

The orange wavelengths reflect off the petals and enter your ______________.

↓

You see the petals as the color ______________.

3. What do you see when white light strikes a material that reflects all the colors, such as a skunk's stripe? ______________________________

____

4. What do you see when white light strikes a material that absorbs all the colors, such as a skunk's body? ______________________________

____

5. Is the following sentence true or false? Objects can look a different color depending on the color of light in which they are seen.

____

6. Circle the letter of the color of light that a red filter allows to pass through it.

a. blue **b.** magenta **c.** cyan **d.** red

▶ Combining Colors (pages 307–309)

7. The three colors that can be used to make any other color are called

_______________.

8. Any two primary colors combined in equal amounts produce

_______________.

9. What are the three primary colors?

a. _______________ **b.** _______________ **c.** _______________

10. When combined in equal amounts, what do the primary colors of light produce? _______________

11. Complete the following "equations" by writing the secondary color the two primary colors of light produce.

a. Green + Blue = _______________

b. Red + Green = _______________

c. Red + Blue = _______________

12. Any two colors of light that combine to form white light are called

_______________.

13. What are pigments? _______________

____

____

14. Complete the following "equations" by writing the secondary color the two primary colors of pigments produce.

a. Magenta + Cyan = ________________

b. Magenta + Yellow = ________________

c. Cyan + Yellow = ________________

SECTION 10-4 Seeing Light (pages 311-314)

This section explains how your eyes allow you to see. It also describes what kinds of lenses are used to correct vision problems.

▶ The Human Eye (pages 312–313)

Match the part of the eye with its description.

	Part of Eye	Description
_____	1. Cornea	a. The hole through which light enters the eye
_____	2. Iris	b. The transparent front surface of the eye
_____	3. Pupil	c. The short, thick nerve through which signals travel to the brain
_____	4. Lens	d. The ring of colored muscle around the pupil
_____	5. Retina	e. The curved part behind the pupil that refracts light
_____	6. Optic nerve	f. The layer of cells lining the inside of the eyeball

7. What do your eyelids do for your eyes each time you blink? ________

____

____

8. What part gives the eye its color? ________________

9. Why does the pupil look black? ________________________

____

10. What is the retina made up of? ______________________________

____

____

11. The cells of the retina that distinguish among black, white, and shades of gray are called ________________.

12. The cells of the retina that respond to colors are called ________________.

13. Label the parts of the eye on the illustration.

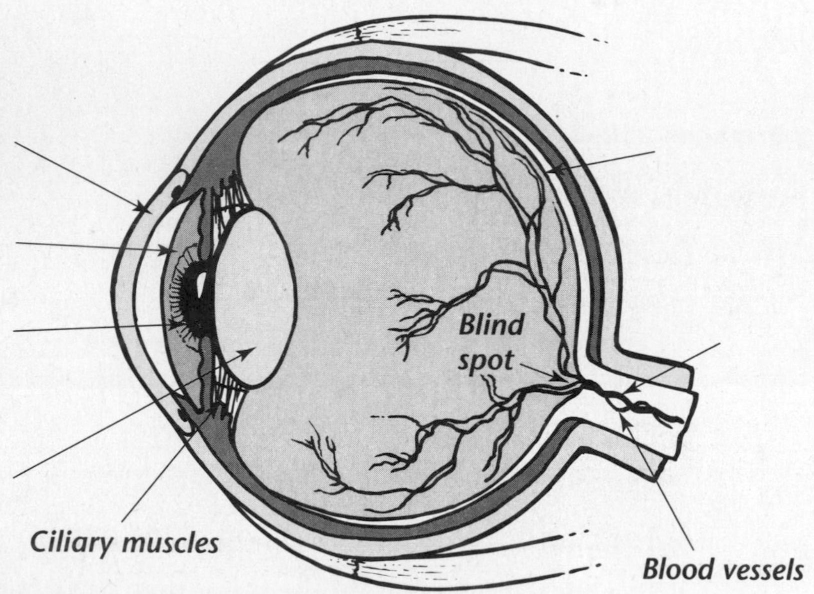

▶ Correcting Vision (pages 313–314)

14. Complete the table about correcting vision.

Correcting Vision			
Vision Problem	**Shape of Eyeball**	**Vision Perception**	**Type of Correction Lens**
Nearsightedness		Distant objects appear blurry	
	A little too short		

Name ______________________ Date __________ Class ______________

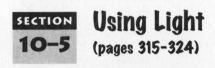

Reading Skill Practice

An outline can help you remember the main points of a section in the order in which they appear. Write an outline of Section 10–4. The title of your outline should be the same as the title of the section. Use the section's major headings for your major topics. Use the section's subheadings for your subtopics. List details about each subtopic under your subheadings. When you finish, you'll have an outline of the section. Do your work on a separate sheet of paper.

SECTION 10–5

Using Light

(pages 315–324)

This section describes how telescopes, microscopes, and cameras work. It also explains how a special kind of light differs from ordinary light.

▶ Telescopes (page 316)

1. An instrument that forms enlarged images of distant objects and makes them appear closer is called a(n) ________________.

2. What is the most common use of telescopes? ______________________

____

3. Complete the table about telescopes.

Kinds of Telescopes		
Type of Telescope	**Lenses or Mirrors?**	**Image You See—Upright or Upside Down?**
	Lenses	
	Mirrors	

4. What does the objective lens of a refracting telescope do? ____________

____

5. What does the eyepiece lens of a refracting telescope do? ______________

____

____

▶ Microscopes (page 317)

6. An instrument that uses a combination of lenses to produce enlarged images of tiny objects is called a(n) ______________.

7. On a microscope, what is the function of the objective lens? ______________

____

____

▶ Cameras (pages 317–318)

8. An instrument that uses lenses to focus light and record an image of an object is called a(n) ______________.

9. What happens when you press the button of a camera? ______________

____

____

10. How is the diaphragm of a camera like the iris of an eye? ______________

____

____

____

▶ Lasers (pages 318–319)

11. What is a device called that produces coherent light, which consists of light waves that all have the same wavelength? ______________

12. In a laser beam, the crests and troughs of all the waves ______________ with each other.

13. What does a laser consist of? ______________________

____

____

▶ Uses of Lasers (pages 320–322)

14. Circle the letter of each sentence that is true about the uses of lasers.
   a. Some lasers are used to cut through steel.
   b. A laser beam is used to play compact discs, or CDs.
   c. A laser beam is used as a tunnel between England and France.
   d. Doctors use lasers in surgery.

15. What is a hologram? ______________________

____

____

▶ Optical Fibers (pages 322–324)

16. Is the following sentence true or false? Laser beams can carry signals by modulation like radio waves. ______________

17. What are optical fibers? ______________________

____

____

18. The complete reflection of light by the inside surface of a medium is called ______________________.

19. Circle the letter of each sentence that is true about the uses of optical fibers.
   a. An optical fiber can carry only one telephone call at a time.
   b. Doctors use optical fibers to examine internal organs.
   c. Optical fibers are much thinner than copper wire.
   d. Optical fibers have led to great improvements in computer networks.

Name ______________________ Date __________ Class ______________

WordWise

Answer the questions by writing the correct key terms in the blanks. Use the circled letter in each term to find the hidden key term. Then write a definition for the hidden key term.

What is a curved piece of glass or other transparent material that is used to refract light? _ _ ◯ _

What is a copy of an object formed by reflected or refracted rays of light?
_ _ _ _ ◯

What is an instrument called that uses lenses to focus light and record an image of an object? _ ◯ _ _ _ _

What is the transparent front surface of the eye called? _ _ ◯ _ _ _

What is a device called that produces coherent light, which consists of light waves that all have the same wavelength? _ _ ◯ _ _

What is an instrument called that uses a combination of lenses to produce enlarged images of tiny objects? _ ◯ _ _ _ _ _ _ _ _

What are substances called that are used to color other materials?
_ _ ◯ _ _ _ _ _

What is a person called who can see distant objects clearly, but nearby objects appear blurry? _ _ _ _ _ _ ◯ _ _ _

What is the layer of cells that line the inside of the eyeball called? _ _ ◯ _ _ _

What is a material called that reflects or absorbs all of the light that strikes it?
_ _ _ _ _ ◯

What is the measure of how much a ray of light bends when it enters the material called? _ _ ◯ _ _   _ _   _ _ _ _ _ _ _ _ _ _

Hidden Term: _ _ _ _ _ _ _ _ _ _ _

Definition: ____

____

Name ______________________ Date __________ Class ______________

CHAPTER 11

MAGNETISM AND ELECTROMAGNETISM

SECTION 11-1 The Nature of Magnetism (pages 336–343)

This sections describes magnets and explains the magnetic force around magnets. It also describes the inside of magnets.

▶ Magnets (page 337)

1. Circle the letter of the mineral that magnetic rocks contain.

a. magnetite **b.** manganese **c.** lodestone **d.** lignite

2. What is magnetism? ______________________________

____

____

▶ Magnetic Poles (pages 337–338)

3. Any magnet, no matter what its shape, has two ends, each one called a(n) ______________.

4. Circle the letter of each sentence that is true about magnetic poles.

a. One pole of a magnet will point north.

b. Both the north and the south pole always point north.

c. Two north poles make up a pair of unlike, or opposite, poles.

d. The pole that points south is labeled the south pole.

5. What happens if you break a magnet in two? ______________________________

____

____

6. Complete the table below by writing whether the magnets in each pair described in the first column will repel or attract each other.

Magnetic Attraction	
Situation	**Repel or Attract?**
Two south poles are brought together.	
A north pole is brought to a south pole.	
Two north poles are brought together.	
A south pole is brought to a north pole.	

▶ Magnetic Fields (pages 339–340)

7. The region of magnetic force around a magnet is known as its

______________________.

8. What are the lines called that map out the magnetic field around a magnet? ______________________

9. Draw a magnetic field around the illustration of the bar magnet shown here.

10. When the magnetic fields of two or more magnets overlap, what is the result? ____

____

Name ______________________ Date ________ Class ______________

▶ Inside a Magnet (pages 340–341)

11. What do the magnetic properties of a material depend on? ____________

____

____

12. The smallest particle of an element that has the properties of that element is called a(n) ______________.

13. One of about 100 basic materials that make up all matter is called a(n) ______________.

14. What is the central core of an atom called? ______________

15. What is the difference between protons and electrons? ______________

____

____

____

16. A cluster of billions of atoms that all have magnetic fields that are lined up in the same way is known as a(n) ______________.

17. How are magnetic domains arranged differently in magnetized material and in material that is not magnetized? ______________

____

____

____

____

18. What is a ferromagnetic material? ______________

____

____

▶ Making Magnets (page 342)

19. What are two ways to make a magnet from an unmagnetized ferromagnetic material? ______________________

____

____

20. A magnet made of a material that keeps its magnetism is called a(n) ______________________.

▶ Destroying Magnets (page 343)

21. What might happen if you drop a permanent magnet or strike it hard?

____

____

____

22. Is the following sentence true or false? Above a certain temperature, a material loses the property of ferromagnetism. ______________

▶ Breaking Magnets (page 343)

23. Suppose you break a magnet into four pieces. What will be the magnetic properties of each piece? ______________________

____

Reading Skill Practice

Writing a summary can help you remember the information you have read. When you write a summary, write only the most important points. Write a summary of the information under the heading *Inside a Magnet* on pages 341–342. Your summary should be shorter than the text on which it is based. Do your work on a separate sheet of paper.

Name ______________________ Date __________ Class ______________

SECTION 11–2

Magnetic Earth

(pages 346–351)

This section identifies the magnetic properties of Earth and describes the effects of Earth's magnetic field.

▶ Introduction (page 346)

1. What is a compass? ____

____

____

2. Which way does a compass needle usually point? ____________________

▶ Earth As a Magnet (page 347)

3. How is Earth like a bar magnet? ____

____

____

4. The poles of a magnetized needle on a compass align themselves with Earth's ______________________.

▶ Magnetic Declination (pages 347–349)

5. Circle the letters of the two answers that name the same place on Earth.
   - **a.** geographic north pole
   - **b.** geographic south pole
   - **c.** magnetic north pole
   - **d.** true north

6. Is the following sentence true or false? The magnetic poles are not located exactly at the geographic poles. ____________________

7. The angle between a line to the geographic north pole and a line to the magnetic north pole is known as ______________________.

▶ The Magnetosphere (pages 349–350)

8. The doughnut-shaped regions 1,000–25,000 kilometers above Earth are called the ______________________.

9. What do the Van Allen belts contain? ______________________

____

10. The stream of electrically charged particles flowing at high speeds from the sun is called the ______________________.

11. Circle the letter of the sentence that explains Earth's magnetosphere.

a. The doughnut-shaped region 1,000 kilometers above Earth

b. The region of Earth's magnetic field shaped by the solar wind

c. The region between the geographic north pole and the magnetic north pole

d. The region of Earth's magnetic field in the Van Allen belts

12. What is an aurora? ______________________

____

13. Complete the flowchart about what causes the Northern Lights.

Particles from the solar wind penetrate Earth's ______________________.

↓

The particles follow the lines of Earth's magnetic field to the magnetic ______________.

↓

When the particles get close to the surface, they interact with atoms in the ______________.

↓

The interaction causes the atoms to give off glowing ______________________.

▶ Effects of Earth's Magnetic Field (pages 350–351)

14. How could Earth's magnetic field magnetize an iron bar over many years?

____

____

____

____

15. The magnetic record in the rock on the ocean floor depends on when the rock was ________________.

16. Is the following sentence true or false? Earth's magnetic field has reversed direction every million years or so. ________________

SECTION 11-3 Electric Current and Magnetic Fields (pages 352–357)

This section explains how an electric current is related to a magnetic field. It also describes some characteristics of electric currents.

▶ Electric Current (pages 352–353)

Match each particle with its electric charge.

	Particle	Electric Charge
______	**1.** electron	**a.** negative
______	**2.** proton	**b.** positive

3. The flow of electric charges through a material is called ________________________.

4. How is the rate at which an electric current flows determined? _______

____

____

5. Circle the letter of each of the following that stands for the unit of current.

   a. A b. ampere c. aurora d. amp

6. Is the following sentence true or false? The number of amps tells the amount of charge flowing past a given point each second.

   ____

7. An electric current produces a(n) ______________________.

8. Look at Figure 17 on page 353. Why are the compass directions different in Figure 17B than in Figure 17C? ______________________

   ____

   ____

   ____

▶ Moving Charge and Magnetism (page 353)

9. What causes all magnetism? ______________________

   ____

▶ Electric Circuits (pages 354–355)

10. What is an electric circuit? ______________________

    ____

11. What are the three basic features all electric circuits must have?

    a. ______________________

    ____

    b. ______________________

    ____

    c. ______________________

    ____

12. What does a source of electrical energy do in an electrical circuit?

____

13. When a switch in an electrical circuit is closed, is the circuit complete or broken? ______________

14. On the circuit diagram shown here, label the switch, the resistor, and the energy source.

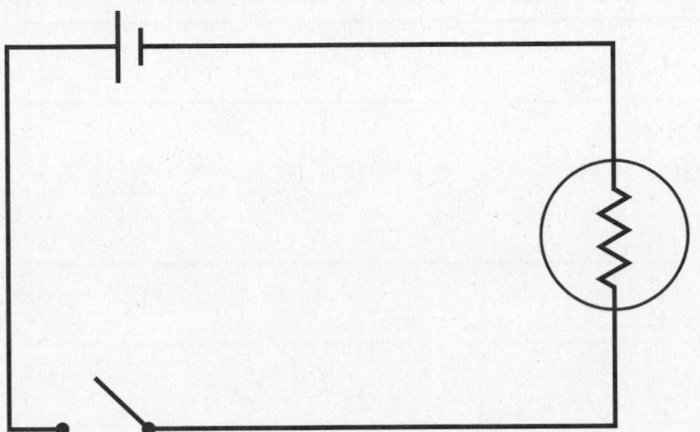

▶ Conductors and Insulators (page 354)

15. Complete the table about conductors and insulators.

Conductors and Insulators		
Material	**Description**	**Examples**
	Electric currents move freely through these materials.	
	Electric currents are not able to move freely through these materials.	

▶ Electrical Resistance (pages 356–357)

16. A device that uses electrical energy as it interferes with, or resists, the flow of charge is called a(n) ______________.

17. Circle the letter of each of the following that could be a resistor in an electrical circuit.

a. computer　**b.** switch　**c.** battery　**d.** light bulb

18. What is resistance? ______________________

____

____

19. Within a material, what results in the conversion of an electron's energy to thermal energy and electromagnetic energy? ______________________

____

____

20. Why did Thomas Edison decide to use tungsten when he developed his electric light bulb? ______________________

____

21. What is a superconductor? ______________________

____

____

SECTION 11–4 Electromagnets (pages 360–362)

This section describes the characteristics of strong magnets that can be turned on and off.

▶ Solenoids (pages 360–361)

1. Is the following sentence true or false? The strength of a magnetic field decreases as the number of loops in a wire increases. ______________________

2. Suppose you wind a current-carrying wire into a coil. How have you changed the wire's magnetic field? ______________________

____

____

3. A current-carrying wire with many loops is called a(n) ________________.

4. How could you turn off a solenoid's magnetic field? ________________

____

▶ Multiplying Magnetism (page 361)

5. Is the following sentence true or false? When iron is placed within a solenoid's magnetic field, the iron becomes a magnet. ________________

6. What is an electromagnet? ________________

____

7. In an electromagnet, what produces the temporary magnetic field?

____

____

▶ Increasing the Strength of An Electromagnet (page 362)

8. Describe three ways you can increase the strength of an electromagnet.

a. ____

____

b. ____

____

c. ____

____

▶ Recording Information (page 362)

9. Is the following sentence true or false? When you record information on a computer disk, you are using electromagnets. ________________

10. When you talk into a microphone, the variations in your voice are changed into variations in a(n) ________________.

Name ______________________ Date __________ Class ______________

WordWise

Complete the crossword puzzle by using the clues below.

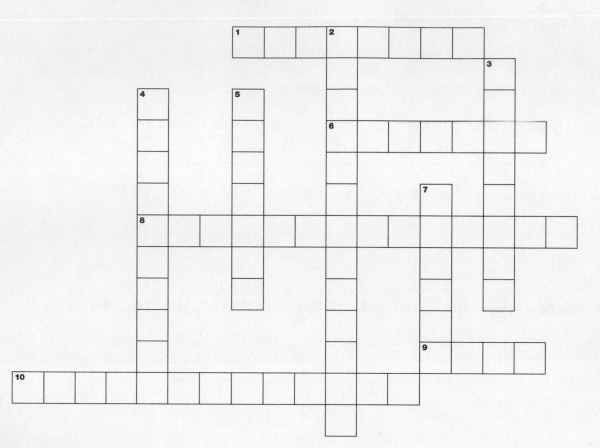

Clues Across

1. A current-carrying coil of wire with many loops
6. A device that has a magnetized needle that can spin freely
8. A material that has no electrical resistance
9. The smallest particle of an element that has the properties of that element
10. The region of Earth's magnetic field shaped by the solar wind

Clues Down

2. A solenoid with a ferromagnetic core
3. A device in an electric circuit that uses electrical energy as it interferes with the flow of electric charge
4. The opposition to the movement of charges flowing through a material
5. The central core of every atom
7. A glowing region of the atmosphere caused by charged particles from the sun

Name ______________________ Date ____________ Class ______________

CHAPTER 12

ELECTRIC CHARGES AND CURRENT

SECTION 12-1 Electric Charge and Static Electricity
(pages 368–375)

This section describes how electric charges interact. It also explains static electricity.

▶ Types of Electric Charge (pages 368–369)

1. Why do protons repel protons but attract electrons? ______________________

____

2. The charge on a proton is called ______________.

3. The charge on an electron is called ______________.

▶ Interactions Between Charges (page 369)

4. Circle the letter of each statement that is true about interactions between charges.

   a. Charges that are the same repel each other.

   b. Charged objects never attract each other.

   c. Charges that are different attract each other.

   d. Charged objects always repel each other.

▶ Electric Fields (pages 369–370)

5. The field around electrically charged particles that exerts a force on other charged particles is called a(n) ______________________.

6. What happens when a charged particle is placed in the electric field of another particle with the same charge? ______________________

____

Name ______________________ Date __________ Class ______________

7. Electric field lines are drawn with arrows to show the direction of the force on a(n) ______________________.

8. Is the following sentence true or false? When two charged particles come near each other, the electric field of only one of the particles is altered. ______________

▶ Static Charge (pages 370–372)

9. Circle the letter of the sentence that explains why there is no overall electrical force in a neutral object.
   a. In the object's atoms, each positive charge is balanced by a negative charge.
   b. The object's atoms contain no charged particles.
   c. The positive charges are attracted to other positive charges.
   d. In the object's atoms, negative charges outnumber positive charges.

10. How can a neutral object become charged? ______________________

____

____

11. If an object gains electrons, what will be its overall charge?

____

12. The buildup of charges on an object is called ______________________.

13. Complete the table about methods of transferring charge.

Transferring Charges	
Method	**Definition**
	The transfer of electrons from one object to another by rubbing
	The movement of electrons to one part of an object by the electric field of another object
	The transfer of electrons from a charged object to another object by direct contact

14. What law states that charges are not created or destroyed? ____________

____

15. Suppose you dry your clothes in a dryer, and when you take them out they cling to one another. Why do they stick together? ____________

____

____

____

▶ Static Discharge (pages 372–374)

16. What happens when a negatively charged object and a positively charged object are brought together? ____________________

____

17. The loss of static electricity as electric charges move off an object is called ____________________.

18. On a humid day, what molecules might carry off extra electrons and prevent the buildup of charges on objects? ____________________

19. Is the following sentence true or false? Lightning is an example of static discharge. ______________

▶ Detecting Charge (page 375)

20. An electric charge can be detected by an instrument called a(n) ______________.

21. Why do the leaves of an electroscope spread apart when a charged object touches the metal knob? ____________________

____

____

____

Reading Skill Practice

A flowchart can help you remember the order in which events occur. On a separate sheet of paper, create a flowchart that describes the steps that take place when lightning reaches Earth, as explained on page 374. The first event in your flowchart will be this: Negative charges on the bottom of a cloud repel electrons. For more information about flowcharts, see page 833 of the Skills Handbook in your textbook. Do your work on a separate sheet of paper.

SECTION 12–2 Circuit Measurements
(pages 378–383)

This section explains what causes an electric current to flow. It also describes what an electric circuit needs to maintain an electric current.

▶ Electrical Potential (page 378)

1. The type of energy that depends on position is called _______________.

2. The potential energy in an electric circuit is related to the force exerted by _______________.

3. What is electrical potential? _______________

____

▶ Voltage (page 379)

4. The difference in electrical potential between two places is called the _______________.

5. What is another name for potential difference? _______________

6. What causes current to flow through an electric circuit?

____

Name ______________________ Date __________ Class ______________

▶ Voltage Sources (page 380)

7. What does a voltage source do in an electric circuit? ________________

____

8. Circle the letter of each example of a voltage source.

   a. light bulb b. generator c. computer d. battery

9. What does an increase in voltage cause in an electric circuit? __________

____

____

10. Charges move around an electric circuit as the result of the potential difference between a voltage source's two ________________.

▶ Resistance (pages 380–381)

11. Circle the letter of the two factors that affect the amount of current that flows through a circuit.

    a. voltage b. resistance c. switch d. current

12. Is the following sentence true or false? The greater the resistance, the less current there is for a given voltage. ________________

13. If an electric current can travel through two paths, which will it travel through? ________________________________

____

▶ Ohm's Law (pages 382–383)

14. A device that measures potential difference, or voltage, is called a(n) ________________.

15. What does an ammeter measure? ________________

16. Is the following sentence true or false? The resistance of most conductors does not vary with the amount of voltage across them.

____

17. What is the formula for Ohm's law?

____

18. If you know the current and the resistance in a circuit, what formula would you use to find the voltage? ____________________

19. Write the unit of measure and its abbreviation for each value.

resistance: ____________________

voltage: ____________________

current: ____________________

20. Circle the letter of each sentence that is true if the resistance of a conductor remains constant.

a. The greater the voltage, the greater the current.

b. The greater the current, the greater the voltage.

c. The greater the voltage, the less the current.

d. The greater the current, the less the voltage.

21. If you double the resistance of a conductor, what happens to the current? ____________________

22. Why are resistors sometimes added to circuits? ____________________

____

SECTION 12–3 Series and Parallel Circuits
(pages 386–389)

This section describes the parts of an electric circuit and identifies two types of circuits.

▶ Series Circuits (page 387)

1. If all the parts of an electric circuit are connected one after another, the circuit is called a(n) ____________________.

2. In a series circuit, how many paths are there for a current to take?

____

3. Suppose you have a number of light bulbs connected together in a series circuit. What happens if one of the bulbs burns out? _______________

____

____

4. As more light bulbs are added to a series circuit, the bulbs become dimmer. Why? _______________

____

____

____

5. If you wanted to measure the current through some device in a circuit, how would you connect an ammeter? _______________

____

▶ Parallel Circuits (pages 387–388)

6. If different parts of a circuit are on separate branches, the circuit is called a(n) _______________.

7. Suppose you have a number of light bulbs connected on a circuit, with each bulb on a separate branch. What happens if one of the bulbs burns out?

____

____

____

8. Circle the letter of each sentence that is true about what happens when more branches are added to a parallel circuit.

   a. Resistance increases.
   b. The current has more paths to follow.
   c. Resistance decreases.
   d. The current has fewer paths to follow.

9. Is the following sentence true or false? Adding more paths to a parallel circuit will increase the current. _______________

10. Identify each of the circuits shown here by writing the type of circuit on the line.

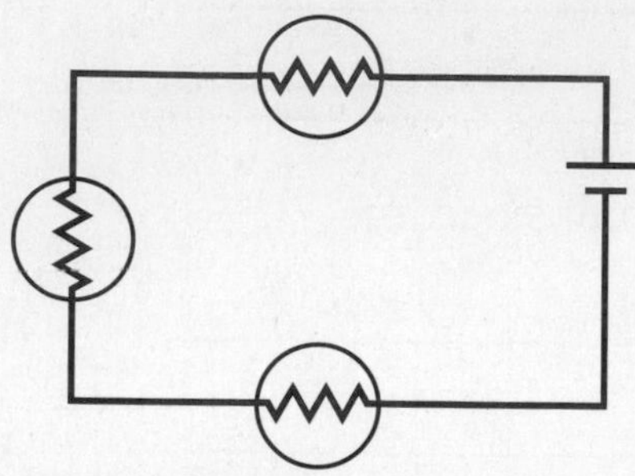

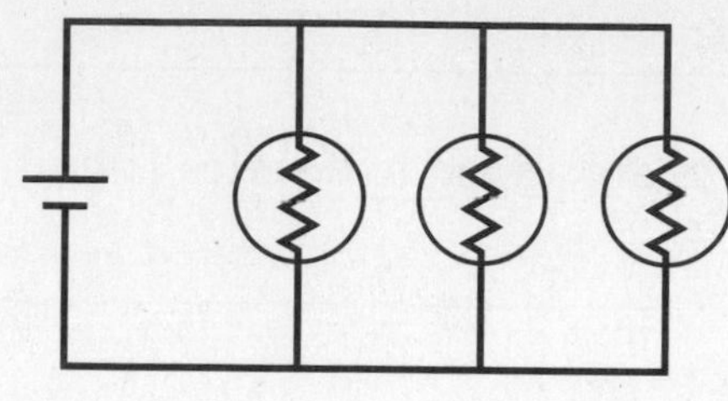

_______________ _______________

▶ Household Circuits (page 389)

11. Why wouldn't you want the circuits in your home to be series circuits?

____

____

12. What kind of circuit carries current to wall sockets and appliances in a home? _______________

13. The voltage in household circuits is _______________.

SECTION 12–4 Electrical Safety

(pages 390–394)

This section describes safety devices used to protect people from the dangers of electricity. It also identifies important rules to follow when using electricity.

▶ Becoming Part of a Circuit (pages 390–391)

1. What is a short circuit? ____

____

2. If you touch your hand to a 120-volt circuit, a potential difference is created between your hand and ______________.

3. Why is it dangerous when the insulation wears off of a wire? ______________

____

____

____

▶ Grounding (pages 391–392)

4. The round prong of a plug that connects the metal shell of an appliance to the ground wire of a building is called the ______________.

5. Circle the letter of the sentence that explains what it means when a circuit is electrically grounded.

   a. Charges always flow from the intended path to the unintended path.

   b. Short circuits move through the ground instead of through water.

   c. Resistance increases throughout a parallel circuit in the event of a short circuit.

   d. Charges are able to flow directly from the circuit into the ground connection in the event of a short circuit.

6. What is a lightning rod? ______________

____

7. When lightning hits a lightning rod, what is the path of the current that results? ______________

____

8. If you are outside during a thunderstorm, would it be safe to hold an umbrella with a pointed rod through the top? Explain. ______________

____

____

____

▶ Fuses and Circuit Breakers (pages 392–393)

9. Electric current can become too high if a circuit is overloaded. What might happen if a circuit is overloaded? ______________________

____

____

10. In order to prevent circuits from overheating, what are added to circuits?

____

____

11. Complete the table about fuses and circuit breakers.

Fuses and Circuit Breakers		
Device	**What Happens When Overloaded**	**To Restore Electricity to Circuit**
	Metal strip melts.	
	Electromagnet shuts off circuit.	

▶ Electric Shocks (pages 393–394)

12. Why might an electric shock affect your heart? ______________________

____

____

____

13. Circle the letter of each of the following that you should *never* do.

a. Use a wire with good insulation on it.

b. Turn on a radio when you're standing in water.

c. Try to repair a toaster while it's still plugged in.

d. Handle a plug with a third prong on it.

Name ______________________ Date __________ Class ______________

WordWise

Match each definition in the left with the correct term in the right column. Then write the number of each term in the appropriate box below. When you have filled in all the boxes, add up the numbers in each column, row, and two diagonals. All the sums should be the same.

A. The movement of electrons to one part of an object by the electric field of another object

B. A device that contains a thin strip of metal that will melt if too much current flows through it

C. The difference in electrical potential between two places

D. The transfer of electrons from a charged object to another object by direct contact

E. An electric circuit with only one path for current to take

F. A device that measures current

G. The transfer of electrons from one object to another by rubbing

H. An electric circuit with several paths for current to take

I. A device that measures potential difference

1. fuse
2. friction
3. ammeter
4. voltmeter
5. series circuit
6. induction
7. conduction
8. voltage
9. parallel circuit

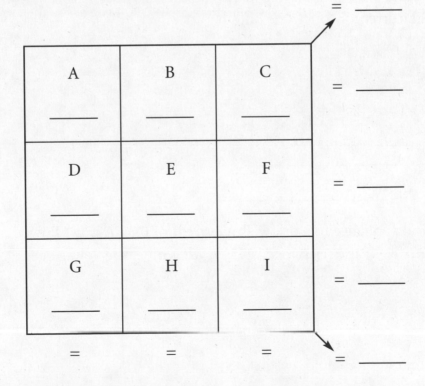

			(diagonal) = _____
A _____	B _____	C _____	= _____
D _____	E _____	F _____	= _____
G _____	H _____	I _____	= _____
= _____	= _____	= _____	(diagonal) = _____

MathWise

For the problems below, show your calculations. If you need more space, use another sheet of paper. Write the answers for the problems on the lines below.

▶ Ohm's Law (pages 382–383)

1. $R = \dfrac{14\text{ V}}{0.2\text{ A}} =$ ______________

2. In a circuit, 15 A is flowing through an electrical appliance. The voltage across the device is 45 V. What is the resistance of the appliance?

   Answer: ______________________

3. $I = \dfrac{12\text{ V}}{30\ \Omega} =$ ______________

4. The voltage across a light bulb is 6.0 V. The bulb's resistance is 15 Ω. What must the current through the bulb be?

   Answer: ______________________

5. $V = 0.60\text{ A} \times 20\ \Omega =$ ______________

6. For an electrical appliance to work well, a current of 0.80 A must flow through its circuits. If the resistance is 25 Ω, what must the voltage be?

   Answer: ______________________

Name ______________________ Date __________ Class ______________

CHAPTER 13

Electricity and Magnetism at Work

SECTION 13–1 Electricity, Magnetism, and Motion (pages 400–403)

This section explains how electrical energy can be converted to mechanical energy. It also describes how an electric motor works.

▶ Electrical and Mechanical Energy (pages 400–401)

1. The ability to move an object some distance is called ________________.

2. Complete the table about forms of energy.

Forms of Energy	
Energy Form	**Definition**
	The energy associated with electric currents
Mechanical energy	

3. When a current-carrying wire is placed in a magnetic field, what energy conversion occurs? ______________________________

____

▶ Galvanometers (pages 401–402)

4. A device that uses an electromagnet to measure small amounts of current is called a(n) ________________.

5. What is used to turn the pointer of a galvanometer?

____

6. In a galvanometer, what does the amount of rotation of the loops of wire and the pointer depend on? ______________________

____

▶ Electric Motors (pages 402–403)

7. A device that uses an electric current to turn an axle is called a(n) ______________________.

8. What energy conversion occurs in an electric motor? ______________________

____

9. A device that reverses the flow of current through an electric motor is called a(n) ______________________.

10. What does a commutator consist of? ______________________

____

11. As a commutator moves, it slides past two contact points called ______________________.

12. The arrangement of wires wrapped around an iron core in an electric motor is called a(n) ______________________.

SECTION 13-2 Generating Electric Current (pages 406–413)

This section explains the production of electric current. It also describes electric generators.

▶ Induction of Electric Current (pages 406–407)

1. The current that results from electromagnetic induction is called a(n) ______________________.

Name ______________________ Date __________ Class ______________

2. When will an electric current be produced in a conductor? ____________

____

____

3. What are two cases in which an electric current can be produced with a conductor and a magnet?

a. ____

b. ____

4. What is electromagnetic induction? ______________________________

____

____

▶ Alternating and Direct Current (pages 407–408)

5. What does the direction of an induced current depend on? __________

____

____

6. Is the following sentence true or false? The flow of an induced current may change direction. ______________

7. Complete the table about induced currents.

Induced Currents			
Induced Current	**Abbreviation**	**Description**	**Example**
	AC		Circuits in the home
	DC		Batteries

▶ Generators (pages 408–409)

8. A device that converts mechanical energy into electrical energy is called a(n) ______________________.

9. How is an electric motor the opposite of an electric generator? ________

____

____

____

10. Is the following sentence true or false? Large generators use armatures similar to those in a motor. ________________

11. The parts of a generator that rotate with the wire loop and make contact with the brushes are called ________________.

▶ Turbines (pages 409–411)

12. Complete the table about energy resources. See *Exploring Energy Resources* on pages 410–411.

Energy Resources		
Resource	**Source of Energy**	**What Turns a Turbine**
	Energy in atom's nucleus	
Hydroelectricity	Falling water	Moving water
Solar energy		Steam
	Movement of tides	
	Heated underground water	
Energy from wind		Windmill
	Chemical energy in fossil fuels	

Name _______________ Date _______ Class _______________

13. A circular device made up of many blades that is turned by water, wind, steam, or tides is called a(n) _______________.

▶ Generating Electricity (pages 412–413)

14. According to the graph in Figure 9 on page 412, what is the leading resource for generating electricity in the United States?

____

15. What percentage of electricity does nuclear energy generate?

____

16. Is the following sentence true or false? Cost is a very important factor in the generation of electricity. _______________

17. According to Figure 10 on page 412, what are the pros of using coal?

____

18. What are three cons of using coal to produce electricity?

a. _______________

b. _______________

c. _______________

19. Which energy resources have pros of "no wastes"? _______________

____

20. Complete the table about energy resources.

Energy Resources		
Type of Resource	**Definition**	**Examples**
	A resource that can be replaced in nature at a rate close to the rate at which it is used	
Nonrenewable resource		

Reading Skill Practice

A graph can help you understand comparisons of data at a glance. Use a piece of graph paper to convert the circle graph in Figure 9 on page 412 into a bar graph. On the graph paper, draw a vertical, or *y*-, axis. The bottom of that line should be labeled 0. The top of the line should be labeled 100%. Then draw a horizontal, or *x*-, axis. Along that line write the names of the energy resources shown in the circle graph. For each resource, draw a solid bar that represents its percentage. For more information about bar graphs, see page 834 in the Skills Handbook of your textbook.

SECTION 13-3 Using Electric Power (pages 414–420)

This section explains how you can calculate power and energy use. It also explains how voltage can be increased or decreased.

▶ Electric Power (page 415)

1. What is power? ______________________________

____

2. The power used by a light bulb or an appliance depends on what two factors?

a. ______________ b. ______________

3. What formula do you use to calculate power?

____

4. Use Figure 13 on page 415 to rank the following appliances according to how much power they use. Rank the appliance with the highest power rating as *1*.

_____ a. toaster
_____ b. microwave oven
_____ c. clothes dryer
_____ d. water heater
_____ e. color television
_____ f. stove

Name ______________________ Date __________ Class ______________

▶ Paying for Energy (page 416)

5. What two factors does the energy use on an electric bill depend on?

   a. ______________

   b. ______________

6. What formula do you use to determine the amount of energy used by an appliance?

   ____

7. Electric power is usually measured in thousands of watts, or

   ______________________.

8. The unit of electrical energy is the ______________________.

9. What is the specific energy equation you would use to determine the amount of electrical energy used by an appliance?

   ____

▶ Transformers (pages 416–417)

10. A device that increases or decreases voltage is called a(n)

    ______________.

11. Why is a transformer necessary so that electricity can be brought into a home? ____

    ____

    ____

    ____

12. In a transformer, what induces a current in the secondary coil? ________

    ____

    ____

    ____

13. Why won't a transformer work with direct current? ______________

____

____

____

▶ Changing Voltage (pages 417–418)

14. If there are more loops in the secondary coil of a transformer than in the primary coil, will the voltage in the secondary coil be higher or lower than in the primary coil? ______________

15. Complete the table below about types of transformers.

Types of Transformers		
Type of Transformer	**Increases or Decreases Voltage?**	**Setup**
		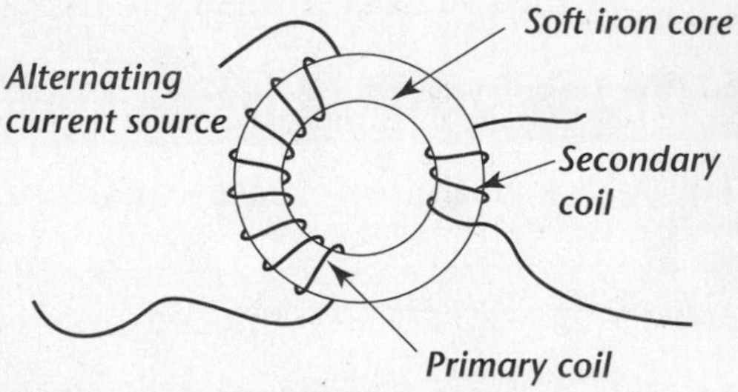 *Soft iron core* *Alternating current source* *Secondary coil* *Primary coil*
		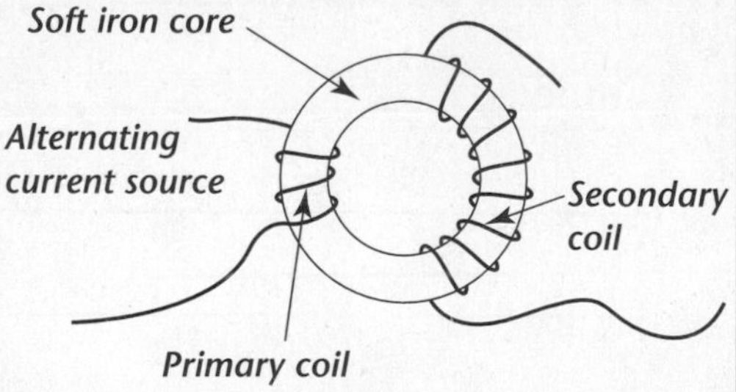 *Soft iron core* *Alternating current source* *Secondary coil* *Primary coil*

▶ The War of the Currents (pages 418–420)

16. Why did Nikola Tesla think AC would be better for distribution of electricity to homes? ______________

____

____

17. What does using alternating current with transformers reduce in long transmission wires? ______________________

18. In Figure 17 on page 420, what hangs on the telephone pole just outside the house? What is the purpose of that device? ______________________

____

____

____

SECTION 13-4 Batteries (pages 421-425)

This section explains how chemical reactions can generate electricity. It also describes how some batteries can be recharged.

▶ The First Battery (pages 422–423)

1. The energy stored in chemical compounds is called ______________________.

2. What is a chemical reaction? ______________________

____

____

3. In the year 1800, who designed the first electric battery?

____

4. In Volta's battery, a chemical reaction between which two metals produced a current? ______________________

▶ Electrochemical Cells (pages 423–424)

5. A device that converts chemical energy into electrical energy is called a(n) ______________________.

CHAPTER 13, Electricity and Magnetism at Work *(continued)*

Match the term with its description.

	Term	Definition
______	6. electrode	a. The part used to connect the cell to a circuit
______	7. electrolyte	b. A metal in an electrochemical cell
______	8. terminal	c. A substance that conducts electric current

9. What occurs between the electrodes and the electrolyte in an electrochemical cell? ______________________

10. How do the chemical reactions change the electrodes? ______________________

____

▶ Dead and Rechargeable Batteries (page 425)

11. A combination of two or more electrochemical cells in a series is called a(n) ______________.

12. Is the following sentence true or false? The voltage of a battery is the sum of the voltages of the cells. ______________

13. Two or more electrochemical cells are connected in a(n) ______________.

14. Complete the table about wet and dry cells.

Electrochemical Cells		
Type of Cell	**Electrolyte—Liquid or Dry?**	**Example**
Wet cell		
	Dry	Flashlight battery

15. A battery in which the products of the electrochemical reaction can be turned back into reactants to be reused is called a(n) ______________.

Name ______________________ Date __________ Class ______________

WordWise

Solve the clues by filling in the blanks with key terms from Chapter 13. Then write the numbered letters in the correct order to find the hidden message.

Clues	Key Terms
An electrochemical cell in which the electrolyte is a liquid	_ _ _ _ _ _ _ 1 (first blank)
The arrangement of wires wrapped around an iron core in an electric motor	_ _ _ _ _ _ _ _ 2 (fourth blank)
A substance that conducts electric current	_ _ _ _ _ _ _ _ _ _ _ 3 (fifth blank)
A current consisting of charges that flow in one direction only	_ _ _ _ _ _ _ _ _ _ _ _ _ 4 (sixth blank)
A device that increases or decreases voltage	_ _ _ _ _ _ _ _ _ _ _ 5 (fifth blank)
A device that uses an electromagnet to measure small amounts of current	_ _ _ _ _ _ _ _ _ _ _ _ 6 (fourth blank)
A metal in an electrochemical cell	_ _ _ _ _ _ _ _ _ 7 (seventh blank)
An electrochemical cell in which the electrolyte is a paste	_ _ _ _ _ _ _ 8 (sixth blank)
A transformer that decreases voltage	_ _ _ _ - _ _ _ _ 9 (second blank)
The contact points connected to a commutator of an electric motor	_ _ _ _ _ _ _ 10 (fourth blank)
A combination of two or more electrochemical cells in a series	_ _ _ _ _ _ _ 11 (second blank)
A device that reverses the flow of current through an electric motor	_ _ _ _ _ _ _ _ _ _ 12 (fourth blank)
The rate at which energy is converted from one form into another	_ _ _ _ _ 13 (first blank)
The parts of a generator that rotate with the wire loop and make contact with the brushes	_ _ _ _ _ _ _ _ _ 14 (last blank)

Hidden Message

_ _ _ _ _ = _ _ _ _ _ × _ _ _ _

1 2 3 4 5 = 6 7 8 9 10 × 11 12 13 14

MathWise

For the problems below, show your calculations. If you need more space, use another sheet of paper. Write the answers for the problems on the lines below.

▶ Calculating Power (page 415)

1. Power = 120 volts × 4 amps = ______________

2. A boombox uses six 1.5-volt batteries in series to create a current of 0.4 amps. What is the power rating of the radio?

   Answer: ______________________

3. Current = $\frac{60 \text{ watts}}{120 \text{ volts}}$ = ______________

4. A guitar amplifier has a power rating of 180 watts and uses a standard voltage of 120 volts. What is the current through the guitar amplifier?

   Answer: ______________________

▶ Calculating Electrical Energy (page 416)

5. Electrical energy = 4 kilowatts × 6 hours = ______________

6. You dry four pairs of jeans in a clothes dryer for 2 hours. A clothes dryer has a power rating of 5,400 watts. How much electrical energy did you use to dry your jeans?

   Answer: ______________________________

Name ______________________ Date __________ Class ______________

CHAPTER 14

AN INTRODUCTION TO MATTER

SECTION 14-1

Describing Matter
(pages 438–445)

This section describes the three states of matter and the characteristic properties of matter. It also explains how matter can be classified.

▶ Properties of Matter (pages 438–439)

1. Is the following sentence true or false? Matter can be of any shape, any texture, and any color. ________________

2. What are the three principal states of matter?

   a. ________________ b. ________________ c. ________________

▶ Characteristic Properties (pages 439–440)

3. What are characteristic properties of matter? ____

____

4. Circle the letter of the reason why characteristic properties can be used to identify unknown substances.
   - **a.** For a given substance they never change.
   - **b.** Some properties are true only for a given sample of matter.
   - **c.** For a given substance no properties hold true.
   - **d.** There are only three principal states of matter.

5. The temperature at which a liquid boils is called its ________________________.

6. Water, chloroform, and ethanol are all clear, colorless liquids. What could you do to identify an unknown liquid as one of these three?

____

____

____

7. The temperature at which a solid melts is called its

_______________________.

8. Why must you study at least two or three characteristic properties before you can accurately identify a substance? _______________

____

____

____

9. Is the following sentence true or false? Neither boiling point nor melting point can be considered characteristic properties of matter.

____

▶ Changes in Matter (page 441)

10. What are physical changes? _______________________

____

____

11. What are chemical changes? _______________________

____

____

12. The ability to undergo a chemical change is a characteristic property called the _______________________ of a substance.

Name ______________________ Date __________ Class ______________

13. Complete the table by classifying each change as either a physical change or a chemical change.

Changes in Matter	
Change	**Physical or Chemical Change?**
Wood burns	
Soda can is crushed	
Orange juice is filtered	
Sugar is changed into caramel	
Water boils away	

▶ Types of Matter (page 442)

14. Complete the concept map about types of matter.

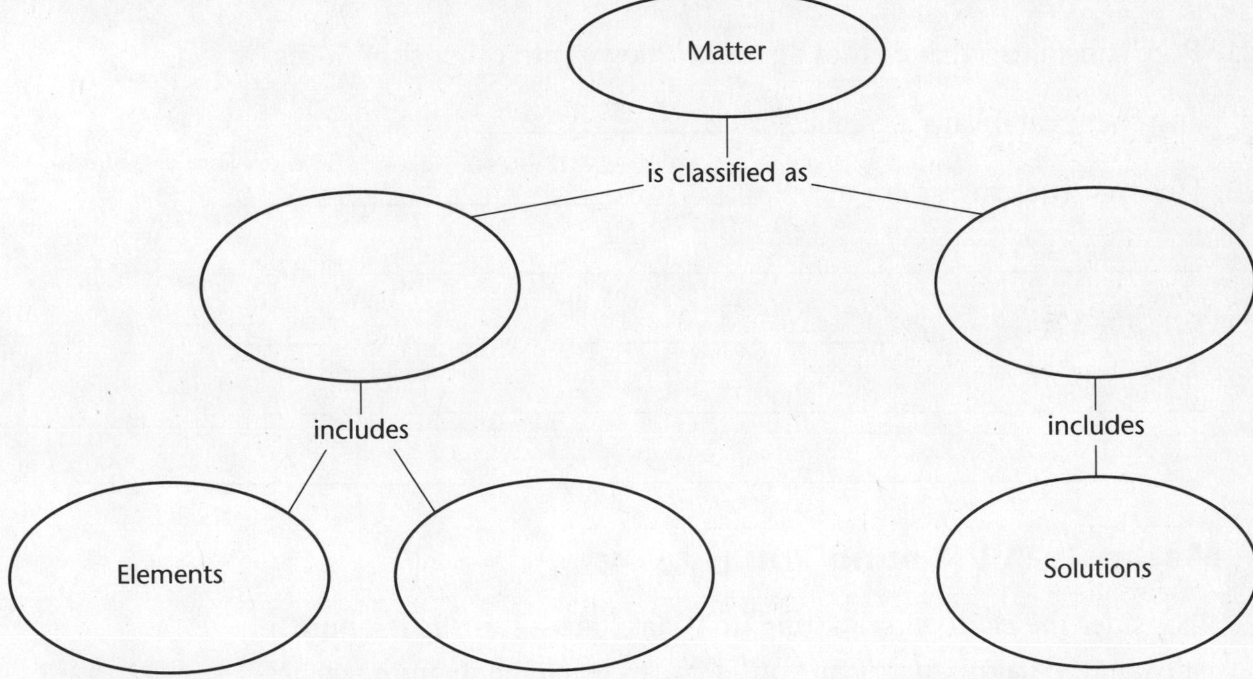

▶ Mixtures (page 442)

15. What does a mixture consist of? ______________________

____

____

CHAPTER 14, An Introduction to Matter *(continued)*

16. When substances are in a mixture, what does each substance keep?

____

17. The “best-mixed” of all mixtures is called a(n) ________________.

18. What are two examples of a solution?

a. ________________ b. ________________

▶ Pure Substances (pages 443–445)

19. A substance made of only one kind of matter and having definite properties is called a(n) ________________.

20. Is the following sentence true or false? Water is not a pure substance because it changes every time it's mixed with something else.

____

21. Pure substances that cannot be broken down into other substances by any chemical means are called ________________.

22. How many elements are there? ________________

____

23. What is a compound? ________________

____

____

▶ Matter Is All Around You (page 445)

24. Consider the chair you're sitting in. What state is it in? Is it a pure substance or a mixture? Can you identify any elements in the chair?

____

____

____

Name ______________________ Date __________ Class ______________

SECTION 14–2

Measuring Matter
(pages 446–451)

This section explains the difference between mass and weight. It also explains what the density of a substance is.

▶ Mass (pages 446–447)

1. A measure of the force of gravity on an object is called ________________.

2. Why would you weigh less on the moon than you do on Earth? ________

____

____

3. What is mass? ____

____

4. Why do scientists rely on mass rather than weight as the measurement of how much matter an object contains? ________________________

____

____

5. What system of units do scientists use to measure the properties of matter?

____

6. The SI unit for mass is ________________.

▶ Volume (pages 447–449)

7. The amount of space that matter occupies is called its ________________.

8. What formula do you use to find the volume of a rectangular object?

____

9. What are the SI/metric units for volume listed in Figure 9 on page 450?

a. ____________________ **b.** ____________________

c. ____________________ **d.** ____________________

▶ Density (pages 450–451)

10. What is density? ______________________________

____

11. Why does a kilogram of bricks take up a much smaller space than a kilogram of feathers? ______________________________

____

12. What formula do you use to calculate the density of an object?

____

13. One unit of density is g/cm^3. How do you say that unit in words?

____

14. What unit of measurement is used for the density of liquids?

____

15. If you drop a block of gold and a block of wood into water, the gold sinks and the wood floats. What can you conclude about the density of gold and wood compared to the density of water? ______________

____

____

16. Is the following sentence true or false? The density of a substance varies with the samples of that substance. ______________

Reading Skill Practice

Outlining is a way to help yourself understand and remember what you have read. Write an outline of Section 14–2, Measuring Matter. In your outline, copy the headings in the textbook. Under each heading, write the main idea. Then list the details that support, or back up, the main idea. Do your work on a separate sheet of paper.

Name ______________________ Date ____________ Class ______________

SECTION 14–3

Particles of Matter

(pages 453–457)

This section explains what atoms are and describes how scientists model atoms today.

▶ Atoms (page 454)

1. The smallest particles of an element are called ______________________.

▶ Democritus (page 454)

2. Who was Democritus? ______________________

3. Why did Democritus call the smallest piece of matter *atomos*? ______________________

____

▶ Dalton's Ideas (page 455)

4. Who was John Dalton? ______________________

____

5. Complete the table about characteristics of atoms.

Atoms	
Characteristic	**Result**
Atoms can't be broken down into ______________________.	Atoms are nearly impossible to break apart.
In any element, all atoms are ______________________.	An element always has the same properties.
Atoms of two or more elements can combine to form ______________________.	Compounds break down into elements.
Atoms of each element have a unique ______________________.	The atoms of any element have an identifiable mass.
The masses of elements in a compound are always in a(n) ______________________.	In any sample of a compound, the ratio of the masses of elements is always the same.

▶ Atoms and Molecules Today (pages 456–457)

6. Circle the letter of the term that means a group of atoms that are joined together and act as a single unit.
   a. atom
   b. solution
   c. molecule
   d. particle
7. What is the force that holds two atoms together?

   ____
8. Is the following sentence true or false? Molecules can contain as many as a billion atoms. ______________
9. With what tool did scientists capture the image of silicon atoms, as shown in Figure 15 on page 457? ______________________________
10. When you think about matter in terms of atoms and molecules, you are using a model known as the ______________________________.

SECTION 14-4

Elements From Earth
(pages 458–462)

This section explains how the density of gold allows it to be separated from other substances. It also describes how copper and iron can be separated from rocks that contain them.

▶ Gold and Density (page 459)

1. Why can density be used to separate gold from surrounding material?

   ____

   ____

   ____

2. What is gold's density compared to pyrite? ______________________

____

____

3. Today, gold mining is done with big machines called ______________.

▶ Copper and Electrolysis (pages 459–461)

4. How is copper most often found in nature? ______________________

____

____

5. What is an ore? ______________________________________

____

6. What characteristic property of copper is used to extract it from copper ore? ______________________________________

7. A process by which an electric current breaks a chemical bond is called ______________.

8. Complete the flowchart about the electrolysis of an ore.

Copper Electrolysis

A battery produces a(n) ______________________.

↓

The current flows through wire to ______________________,

which are in a solution made of the ______________________.

↓

One electrode attracts the ______________________ of the ore, while the other attracts other components.

↓

The ______________________ is scraped off and used.

Name ______________________ Date __________ Class ______________

▶ Iron and Chemical Activity (page 462)

9. What materials are placed into a hot fire to release iron? ______________

____

____

10. Where does the carbon that is used to purify iron come from? __________

____

____

____

11. What characteristic property of both iron and carbon is utilized to purify iron metal? ______________________

12. Complete the flowchart about how purified iron is produced.

Miners mine iron ____________________, or rocks that contain iron chemically combined with other elements.

↓

Chunks of iron ore and a material called ____________________ are placed in a(n) ____________________ furnace.

↓

At very high temperatures, the ____________________ in the coke reacts with the ____________________ in the iron ore.

↓

The result of the chemical reactions in the blast furnace is purified ____________________.

↓

The purified iron is then mixed with other elements to make ____________________.

Name ______________________ Date __________ Class ______________

WordWise

Complete the following paragraphs using the list of words and phrases below. Each word or phrase may be used only once.

Word Bank

atoms boiling point density molecule elements weight
mixture melting point mass chemical bond compound solution
pure substance chemical properties volume chemical activity

Some properties of matter, such as size or amount, are true only for a given sample of matter. But ______________________ hold true for a particular kind of substance no matter what the sample. One characteristic property is the temperature at which a liquid boils, called the ______________________. Another is the temperature at which a solid melts, called the ______________________. A third characteristic property is ______________________, a substance's ability to undergo chemical change.

Matter can be classified into mixtures and pure substances. A(n) ________________ consists of two or more substances that are mixed together but not chemically combined. The "best-mixed" of all possible mixtures is called a(n) ________________. A(n) ________________ is made of only one kind of matter and has definite properties. Some pure substances, called ________________, cannot be broken down into other substances by any chemical means. A pure substance formed from chemical combinations of two or more elements is a(n) ________________.

The smallest particles of elements are called ________________. Atoms can combine to form different compounds. A group of atoms that are joined together and act as a single unit is a(n) ________________. The force that holds two atoms together is called a(n) ______________________.

There are all sorts of ways of measuring matter. The measurement of the force of gravity on an object is ________________. The measurement of how much matter an object contains is ________________. The measurement of the amount of space that matter occupies is ________________. The measurement of how much mass is contained in a given volume is ________________.

MathWise

For the problems below, show your calculations. If you need more space, use another sheet of paper. Write the answers for the problems on the lines below.

▶ Calculating Volume of a Rectangular Object (page 448)

1. Volume = 10 cm × 5 cm × 6 cm = ______________

2. A box has a length of 25 centimeters, a width of 8 centimeters, and a height of 12 centimeters. What is its volume?

   Answer: ______________

▶ Calculating Density (pages 450–451)

3. Density = $\frac{24\text{ g}}{8\text{ cm}^3}$ = ______________

4. A sample of water has a mass of 13 grams and a volume of 13 milliliters. What is the density of water?

   Answer: ______________

5. A sample of metal has a mass of 94.5 grams and a volume of 7 cubic centimeters. What is its density?

   Answer: ______________

6. A sample of liquid has a mass of 26 grams and a volume of 20 milliliters. What is its density?

   Answer: ______________

Name ______________________ Date __________ Class ______________

CHAPTER 15

Changes in Matter

SECTION 15-1 Solids, Liquids, and Gases (pages 468–472)

This section explains how shape, volume, and the motion of particles are useful in describing solids, liquids, and gases.

▶ Solids (pages 469–470)

1. Which state of matter has a definite volume and a definite shape?

____

2. Is the following sentence true or false? A solid will keep its volume and its shape in any position and in any container. _______________

3. Why do solids have a definite shape and a definite volume? __________

____

____

____

4. Complete the table about types of solids.

Solids			
Type of Solid	**Description**	**Examples**	**Melting Point**
	Made up of crystals		Distinct melting point
	Particles not arranged in a regular pattern		No distinct melting point

5. Circle the letter of each sentence that is true about particles in a solid.
   a. They are completely motionless.
   b. They stay in about the same position.
   c. They vibrate back and forth.
   d. They switch positions occasionally.

▶ Liquids (pages 470–471)

6. Which state of matter has no definite shape but does have a definite volume? ______________

7. Is the following sentence true or false? A liquid's volume does not change no matter the shape of the container. ______________

8. A substance that flows is called a(n) ______________.

9. Circle the letter of the term that means the resistance of a liquid to flowing.
   a. amorphous
   b. solid
   c. viscosity
   d. insulator

10. Is the following sentence true or false? Liquids with high viscosity flow quickly. ______________

▶ Gases (pages 471–472)

11. Which state of matter has neither definite shape nor volume?

    ____

12. If you put a gas into a container with a top, what will the gas do? ______

    ____

    ____

13. The volume and shape of a gas are determined by its ______________.

14. In the containers below, draw how the particles are arranged in the three states of matter.

Solid

Liquid

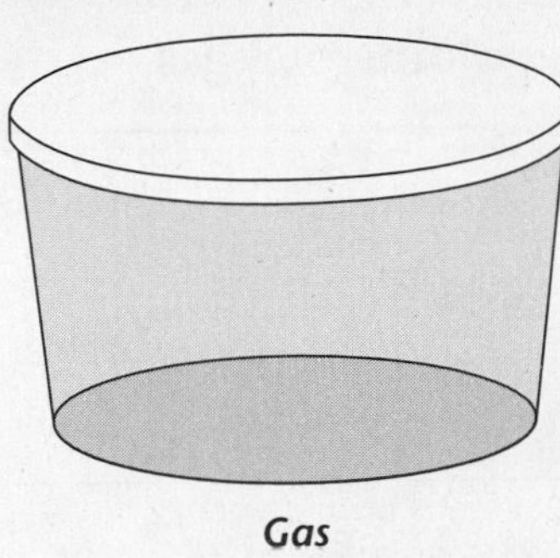
Gas

SECTION 15-2 Behavior of Gases
(pages 473–479)

This section explains how the volume, temperature, and pressure of a gas are related.

▶ Measuring Gases (pages 474–475)

1. The volume of a gas is the same as the volume of its ______________.

2. What is temperature? ______________________________

____

____

3. The force exerted on a surface divided by the total area over which the force is exerted is called ______________.

4. What is the formula you use to calculate pressure?

____

▶ Relating Pressure and Volume (pages 475–476)

5. What does Boyle's law say about the relationship between the pressure and volume of a gas? ______________________________

____

____

6. Complete the table about the relationship between the pressure and volume of a gas.

Pressure and Volume of Gases	
Change	**Increases or Decreases?**
Pressure decreases	Volume
Pressure increases	Volume
Volume increases	Pressure
Volume decreases	Pressure

▶ Relating Pressure and Temperature (pages 476–477)

7. Suppose a gas is kept in a closed, rigid container. If the temperature of the gas increases, what happens to its pressure on the container?

____

____

8. If the temperature of that gas in the container decreases, what happens to its pressure? ______________________________

____

9. How is pressure affected by the collisions of gas particles? __________

____

▶ Volume and Temperature (pages 478–479)

10. What is Charles's law? ______________________________

____

____

11. Is the following sentence true or false? At higher temperatures, the particles of a gas move slower. ______________

Name ______________________ Date __________ Class ______________

12. If the temperature of a gas decreases, what happens to its volume?

____

____

13. Why does a basketball left outside on a cold winter night become soft and lose its bounce? ______________________________

____

____

____

____

Reading Skill Practice

By looking carefully at photographs and illustrations in textbooks, you can help yourself better understand what you have read. Look carefully at Figure 12 on page 476. What important idea does this illustration communicate? Do your work on a separate sheet of paper.

SECTION 15-3 Graphing Gas Behavior
(pages 480–483)

This section describes graphs for Charles's law and Boyle's law.

▶ Introduction (page 480)

1. What is a graph? ______________________________

____

____

2. Is the following sentence true or false? Graphs show how changes in one variable result in changes in a second variable. ______________

▶ Temperature and Volume (pages 481–482)

3. In the experiment represented in Figure 17 on page 481, what is the volume of gas when the temperature is 0°C? ____________

4. When the temperature of the gas rises to 353 kelvins, what is the volume of the gas? ____________

5. On the graph below, label the *x*-axis and the *y*-axis.

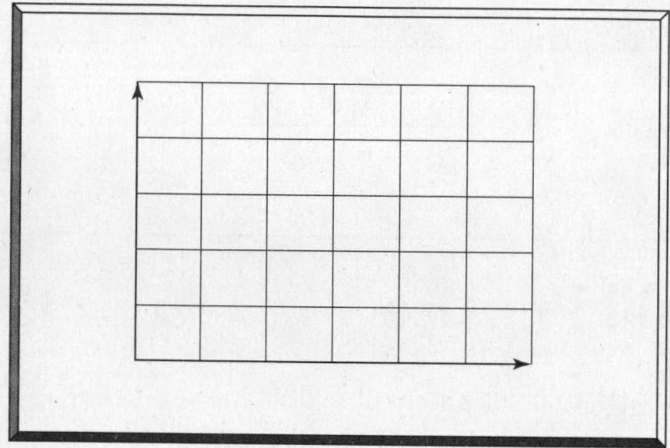

6. Write labels on the graph above that show on which axis the units for the manipulated variable should be placed and on which axis the units for the responding variable should be placed.

7. Where did the data come from that was used to create the graph in Figure 19 on page 482? ____________

8. Compare Figure 18 on page 481 with Figure 19 on page 482. On Figure 19, what is the manipulated variable? ____________

9. What is the responding variable on Figure 19? ____________

10. When a graph of two variables is a straight line passing through the (0,0) point, the relationship is linear and the variables are said to be

______________________ to each other.

11. What does the graph of Charles's law show about the relationship between the temperature and volume of a gas? ______________________

____

____

▶ Pressure and Volume (pages 482–483)

12. In the experiment shown in Figure 20 on page 482, what is the volume and pressure of the gas when the experiment begins? ______________________

____

13. In that experiment, does the pressure increase or decrease as the volume decreases? ______________________

____

14. On the graph in Figure 21 on page 483, what is the manipulated variable and what is the responding variable? ______________________

____

____

15. When a graph of two measurements forms a curve that becomes less steep close to the horizontal axis, the relationship is nonlinear and the measurements are said to ______________________ with one another.

16. What does the graph for Boyle's law show about the relationship between the pressure and volume of a gas? ______________________

____

____

SECTION 15-4 Physical and Chemical Changes
(pages 486–493)

This section explains how physical and chemical changes differ. It also describes changes of state.

▶ Energy and Change (pages 486–487)

1. Complete the table about change.

Changing Matter		
Type of Change	**Definition**	**Example**
Physical change		
Chemical change		

2. The total energy of a substance's particles due to their movement or vibration is called ______________________.

3. The energy stored within the chemical bonds of chemical compounds is called ______________________.

4. Circle the letter of each sentence that is true about changes in matter.
   a. Matter changes whenever energy is added.
   b. Matter changes whenever energy is destroyed.
   c. Matter changes whenever energy is taken away.
   d. Matter changes whenever energy is created.

5. What is the principle called that says that in every physical and chemical change the total amount of energy stays the same? ______________

____

▶ Changes Between Liquid and Solid (page 488)

6. The change in state from a solid to a liquid is called ______________.

7. In most pure substances, melting occurs at a specific temperature called the ______________.

8. The change of state from liquid to solid is called ______________.

9. Is the following statement true or false? The energy loss during the freezing of water changes the arrangement of water's molecules.

____

▶ Changes Between Liquid and Gas (pages 489–490)

10. The change from the liquid to the gas state of matter is called ______________.

11. Complete the concept map.

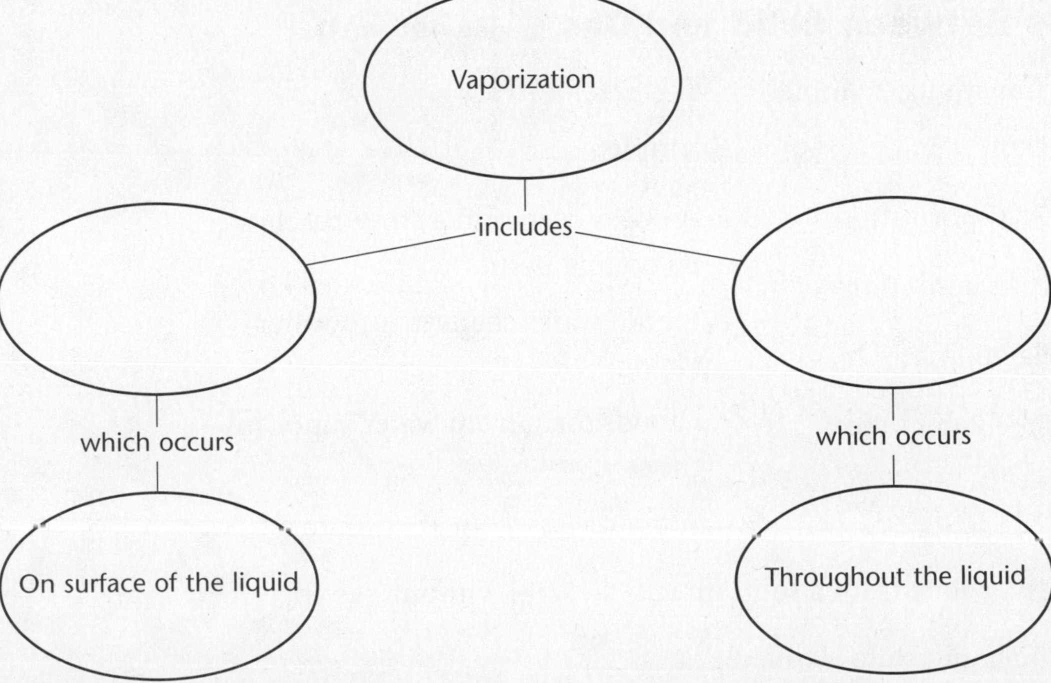

12. Each liquid boils only at a certain temperature, which is called its

______________________.

13. Why is the boiling point of water lower in the mountains than it is at

sea level? ____

____

____

____

____

14. The change in state from a gas to a liquid is called ________________.

15. Is the following sentence true or false? Condensation is the opposite of

vaporization. ______________

16. When condensation occurs, does a gas lose or gain thermal energy?

____

____

▶ Changes Between Solid and Gas (pages 490–491)

Match the term with its example.

Term	Example
______ **17.** vaporization	**a.** A pot of water on a stove reaches its boiling point.
______ **18.** evaporation	**b.** Liquid water changes into water vapor.
______ **19.** boiling	**c.** Clouds form from water vapor in the sky.
______ **20.** condensation	**d.** A puddle dries up after a rain shower.

21. The change of state from a solid directly to a gas without passing

through the liquid state is called ________________.

22. Give an example of sublimation. ______________________________

____

____

▶ Chemical Changes (pages 492–493)

23. Is the following sentence true or false? Changes in state are examples of chemical changes. ______________

24. A process in which substances undergo chemical changes is called a(n) ______________.

25. Circle each sentence that is true about chemical reactions.

   a. All chemical reactions either absorb or release energy.

   b. After a chemical change, the substance is the same as the substance you started with.

   c. In some chemical reactions, two or more substances combine to form new substances.

   d. All chemical reactions produce new substances.

26. Complete the flowchart about energy and chemical reactions in plants.

Plants capture ______________ from the sun.
↓
The plants change energy from the sun into ______________ in the form of various compounds.
↓
The plants are used for food or fuel, and ______________ and ______________ are released through chemical reactions.

27. How can you make a chemical reaction happen faster or slower? ______

____

____

Name ______________________ Date __________ Class ______________

WordWise

The block of letters below contains 11 key terms from Chapter 15. Use the clues to identify the terms you need to find. Then find the terms across, down, or on the diagonal. Circle each term in the hidden-word puzzle.

Clues

The force exerted on a surface divided by the total area over which the force is exerted ______________

The change from the liquid to the gas state of matter ______________

A state of matter with no definite shape or volume ______________

A substance that can flow and easily change shape ______________

The resistance of a liquid to flowing ______________

Vaporization that occurs on and below the surface of a liquid ______________

A state of matter that has no definite shape but has a definite volume ______________

The change in state from a liquid to a solid ______________

A state of matter that has a definite volume and a definite shape ______________

The change in state from a solid to a liquid ______________

A diagram that shows how two variables are related ______________

v	a	p	o	r	i	z	a	t	i	o	n
i	u	r	l	m	l	i	q	u	i	d	f
s	s	e	n	e	y	q	i	d	x	g	r
c	o	s	o	l	i	d	w	n	n	r	e
o	w	s	m	t	p	f	f	i	p	a	e
s	x	u	m	i	a	s	l	d	d	p	z
i	t	r	c	n	a	i	c	u	p	h	i
t	t	e	g	g	o	x	c	i	i	x	n
y	c	i	p	b	t	w	q	m	c	d	g

Name ______________________ Date __________ Class ______________

CHAPTER 16

ELEMENTS AND THE PERIODIC TABLE

SECTION 16–1 Organizing the Elements
(pages 500–510)

This section explains how the elements are organized in a chart called the periodic table. It also explains what information the periodic table contains.

▶ Looking for Patterns in the Elements (page 500)

1. Is the following sentence true or false? All elements easily form compounds with other elements. ______________

▶ Mendeleev, the Detective (page 501)

2. What did Dmitri Mendeleev recognize in 1869? ______________

____

3. What is the atomic mass of an element? ______________

____

____

▶ The First Periodic Table (pages 501–502)

4. Mendeleev noticed that patterns appeared when he arranged the elements in what way? ______________

____

____

5. What does the word *periodic* mean? ______________

____

Name ________________________ Date __________ Class ______________

6. A chart of the elements showing the repeating pattern of their properties is called the ________________________.

▶ The Periodic Table and the Atom (pages 502–505)

7. Circle the letter of each particle that is contained in the nucleus of an atom.

   a. proton **b.** electron **c.** period **d.** neutron

Match the term with its definition.

Term	Definition
______ **8.** nucleus	**a.** Particles outside the nucleus
______ **9.** protons and neutrons	**b.** The number of protons in a nucleus
______ **10.** electrons	**c.** The core of an atom
______ **11.** atomic mass unit	**d.** A unit used in measuring particles in atoms
______ **12.** atomic number	**e.** Particles inside the nucleus

13. Is the following sentence true or false? Every atom of a particular element contains the same number of neutrons. ________________

14. The modern periodic table is now arranged according to ________________________.

▶ Reading the Periodic Table (pages 506–507)

15. A one- or two-letter representation of an element is called a(n) ________________________.

16. Use the square from the periodic table to fill in the blanks below.

Name of element: __________

Chemical symbol: __________

Atomic mass: __________

Atomic number: __________

17. The atomic number for the element calcium (Ca) is 20. How many protons and electrons does each calcium atom have? ______________

____

____

18. How can an element's properties be predicted? ______________

____

____

19. Circle the letter of each term that refers to the elements in a column of the periodic table.

a. period **b.** family **c.** group **d.** symbol

20. Group 15 of the periodic table is the ______________ family.

21. Circle the letter of the statement that is true about elements in each group.

a. They all have the same atomic mass.

b. They all have similar characteristics.

c. They all have similar atomic numbers.

d. They all have the same chemical symbol.

22. Each horizontal row across the periodic table is called a(n) ______________.

23. Is the following sentence true or false? The elements in each period are not alike in properties. ______________

▶ Why the Table Works (pages 508–510)

24. What is bonding power? ______________

____

____

25. Electrons that are involved in sharing between or transfer to other atoms are called ______________.

26. Which electrons of an atom can be shared or transferred? ____________

____

27. Circle the letter of each sentence that is true about valence electrons.

a. All elements have the same number of valence electrons.

b. The number of valence electrons an element has increases from left to right across a period.

c. The number of valence electrons determines whether the element gives up, shares, or accepts electrons.

d. All elements in one group have the same number and arrangement of valence electrons.

Reading Skill Practice

Writing a summary can help you remember the information you have read. When you write a summary, write only the most important points. Write a summary of the information under the heading *Reading the Periodic Table,* pages 506–507. Your summary should be shorter than the text on which it is based. Do your work on a separate sheet of paper.

SECTION 16-2 Metals (pages 511-516)

This section describes the properties of metals and the characteristics of the different groups, or families, of metals.

▶ What Is a Metal (pages 511–512)

1. Chemists classify an element as a metal based on what physical properties? ______________________________

2. Is the following sentence true or false? Most metals are solids at room temperatures because they have the property of very low melting points. ____________

Name ______________________ Date __________ Class ______________

Match the term with its definition.

Term	Definition
______ 3. malleable	a. The ease with which an element combines with other elements and compounds
______ 4. ductile	b. A characteristic of those metals that are attracted to magnets or can be made into magnets
______ 5. magnetic	c. A term used to describe a material that can be pulled out, or drawn, into a long wire
______ 6. reactivity	d. A term used to describe a material that can be pounded or rolled into shape

7. Why are most metals called good conductors? ______________________

____

8. What is the gradual wearing away of a metal element called?

____

▶ Alloys (page 513)

9. A mixture of metals is called a(n) ______________.

10. Bronze is a mixture of what two metals? ______________________

▶ Families of Metals (pages 513–516)

11. How do the properties of each family of metals change as you move across the table? ______________________

____

12. Circle the letter of each sentence that is true about alkali metals.
    - a. They are never found as elements but only in compounds.
    - b. Each atom of an alkali element has one valence electron that is easily transferred.
    - c. They are often found as pure elements in sea water.
    - d. They are extremely reactive.

CHAPTER 16, Elements and the Periodic Table *(continued)*

13. What are the two most important alkali metals?

____

14. Circle the letter of each sentence that is true about alkaline earth metals.

a. Each is a good conductor of electricity.

b. They are never found uncombined in nature.

c. They easily lose their valence electrons in chemical reactions.

d. They are much less reactive than most metals.

15. What are the two most common alkaline earth metals?

____

16. Circle the letter of each element that is a transition metal.

a. gold **b.** iron **c.** copper **d.** lithium

17. Is the following sentence true or false? The transition metals are fairly stable, reacting slowly or not at all with air and water. __________

18. What are the most familiar metals in groups 13 through 16? __________

____

____

19. What is another name for the lanthanides and actinides?

____

20. Where are the lanthanides and actinides found on the periodic table?

____

____

21. Uranium has an atomic number of 92. How were all the elements with atomic numbers higher than 92 created? __________

____

____

22. Complete the concept map about metals.

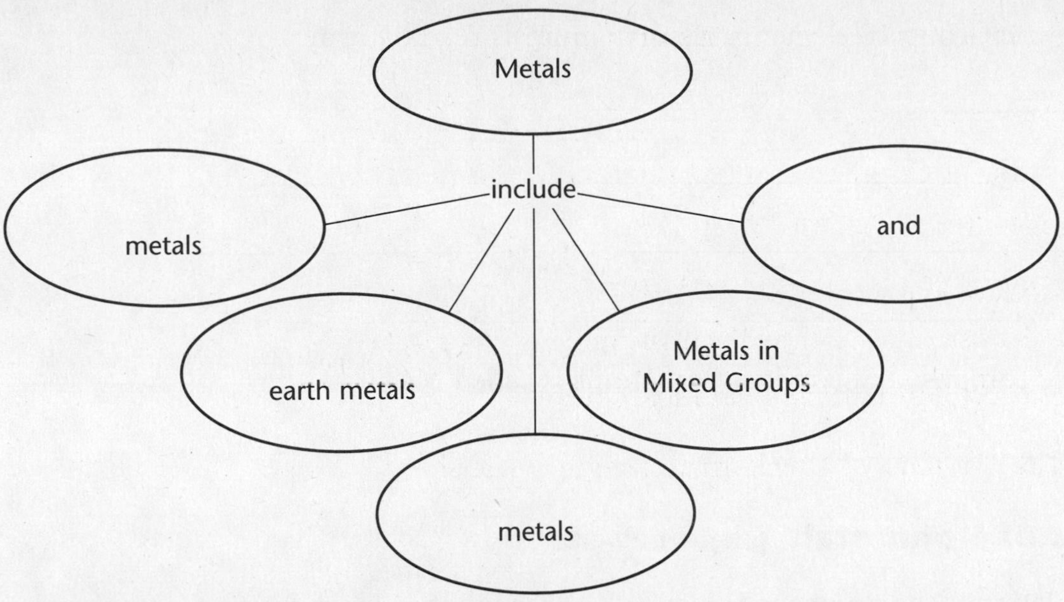

SECTION 16–3 Nonmetals and Metalloids (pages 520–525)

This section describes properties of the elements on the periodic table that are not metals.

▶ What Is a Nonmetal (pages 520–521)

1. The elements that lack most of the properties of metals are called ________________.

2. Where are the nonmetals found on the periodic table? ____

3. Is the following sentence true or false? Many of the nonmetals are gases at room temperature. ________________

4. Circle the letter of each sentence that is true about the physical properties of nonmetals.
   a. Solid nonmetals are brittle.
   b. They usually have lower densities than metals.
   c. Most are shiny.
   d. They are good conductors of both heat and electricity.

5. Except for the Group 18 elements, most nonmetals readily form

_______________.

6. What is a salt? _______________

____

____

7. A molecule composed of two identical atoms is called a(n)

_______________.

▶ Families of Nonmetals (pages 522–525)

8. Circle the letter of the number of valence electrons that an atom in the carbon family has.

   a. 1 **b.** 4 **c.** 5 **d.** 6

9. All living things contain what kind of compounds? _______________

____

____

10. Circle the letter of the number of valence electrons that an atom in the nitrogen family has.

    a. 2 **b.** 7 **c.** 5 **d.** 3

11. The atmosphere is almost 80 percent _______________.

12. Circle the letter of the number of valence electrons that an atom in the oxygen family has.

    a. 6 **b.** 7 **c.** 5 **d.** 2

13. Circle the letter of each sentence that is true about oxygen.

    a. The oxygen you breathe is a diatomic molecule.

    b. Oxygen rarely combines with other elements.

    c. Oxygen is the most abundant element in Earth's crust.

    d. Ozone collects in a layer in the upper atmosphere.

Name ______________________ Date __________ Class ______________

14. Circle the letter of the number of valence electrons that an atom in the halogen family has.

a. 4 **b.** 7 **c.** 6 **d.** 3

15. Is the following sentence true or false? Most halogens are dangerous to humans. ______________

16. Circle the letter of each sentence that is true about the noble gases.

a. They exist in large amounts in the atmosphere.

b. They are chemically very stable and unreactive.

c. They readily share their valence electrons.

d. They are used in glowing electric lights.

17. Complete the table about families of nonmetals.

Nonmetals		
Family	**Group**	**Nonmetals in Family**
Carbon family		
Nitrogen family		
Oxygen family		
Halogen family		
Noble gases		

18. How many protons and electrons does a hydrogen atom contain?

____

____

19. Why can't hydrogen be grouped in a family? ______________

____

____

▶ The Metalloids (page 525)

20. What are metalloids? ____

____

____

21. What is the most common metalloid? ______________________

22. What is the most useful property of the metalloids? ______________________

____

____

23. What are semiconductors? ____

____

____

____

SECTION 16-4 Elements From Stardust (pages 528–530)

This section explains how elements form inside stars.

▶ Atomic Nuclei Collide (pages 528–529)

1. Describe the plasma state of matter. ______________________________

____

____

____

2. The process in which atomic nuclei combine to form a larger nucleus, releasing huge amounts of energy, is called ______________________.

3. What does nuclear fusion create inside stars? ______________________

Name ____________________ Date __________ Class ____________

▶ Elements From the Sun (pages 529–530)

4. What is the major source of energy the sun now produces? ____________

____

____

5. Complete the flowchart about nuclear fusion in stars.

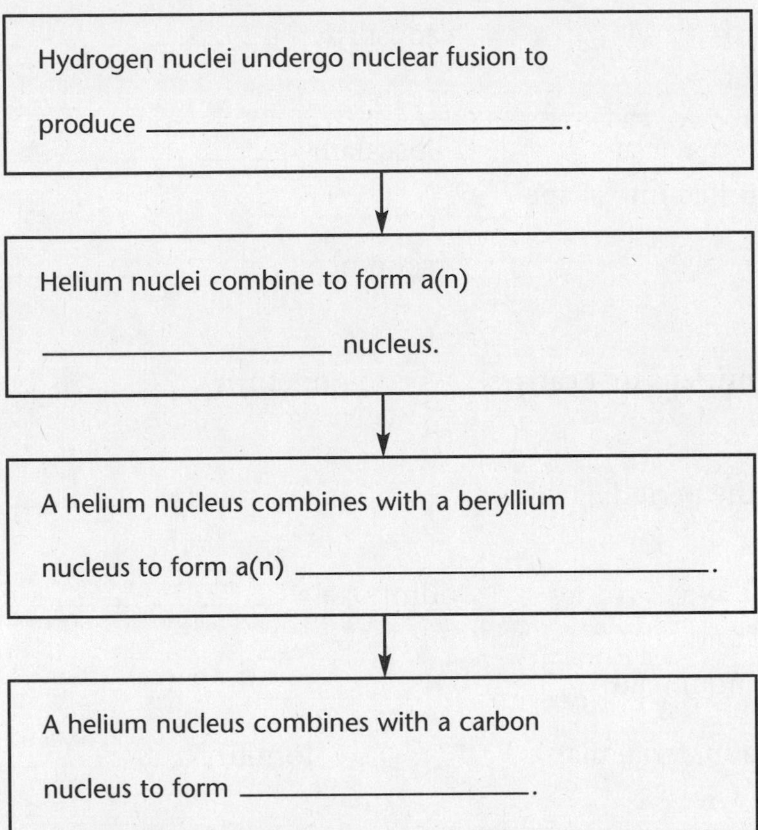

Hydrogen nuclei undergo nuclear fusion to produce ____________.
Helium nuclei combine to form a(n) ____________ nucleus.
A helium nucleus combines with a beryllium nucleus to form a(n) ____________.
A helium nucleus combines with a carbon nucleus to form ____________.

▶ Elements from Large Stars (page 530)

6. In stars more massive than the sun, fusion continues until the core is almost all ____________.

7. What is a supernova? ____________

____

____

8. A supernova provides enough energy for the nuclear fusion reactions that create the ____________.

Name ______________________ Date __________ Class ______________

WordWise

Use the clues to help you unscramble the key terms from Chapter 8. Then put the numbered letters in order to find the answer to the riddle.

Clues	Key Terms	
A tremendous explosion that breaks apart a massive star	eaousprnv	_ _1 _ _ _ _ _ _ _
A term used to describe a material that can be pounded or rolled into shape	llbeealam	_ _ _ _ _2 _ _ _ _
The gradual wearing away of a metal element	rsoooincr	_ _ _3 _ _ _ _4 _ _
A particle in the atomic nucleus that carries no charge	ouetnrn	_ _ _ _ _ _5 _
A horizontal row across the periodic table	roiedp	_ _ _ _ _ _6
An element that has some characteristics of a metal and some characteristics of a nonmetal	ldmtioael	_ _ _ _ _ _ _ _7 _
A term used to describe a material that can be drawn into a long wire	lecuitd	_ _ _8 _9 _ _ _
A state of matter in which atoms are stripped of their electrons and nuclei are packed close together	aamspl	_ _ _10 _ _ _
The elements in Group 18 of the periodic table	beoln ssgea	_ _ _11 _ _ _ _ _ _ _
Elements in the first row of the rare earth elements of the periodic table	sletahnaidn	_12 _ _ _ _ _ _ _ _ _13 _

Riddle: What chart shows the repeating properties of elements?

Answer: _1 _2 _3 _4 _5 _6 _7 _8   _9 _10 _11 _12 _13

Name ______________________ Date __________ Class ____________

CHAPTER 17

CHEMICAL REACTIONS

SECTION 17-1

Matter and Its Changes

(pages 536–541)

This section explains how you can tell when a chemical reaction has occurred. It also describes how chemical bonds are changed in reactions.

▶ Changes in Matter (pages 537–538)

1. What is chemistry? ______________________

____

____

2. What is a physical change? ______________________

____

____

3. Is the following sentence true or false? A change of state is a physical change. ______________

4. What is a chemical change? ______________________

____

____

5. Circle the letter of each sentence that describes a chemical change.

a. Two elements combine to make a compound.

b. A compound is broken down into elements.

c. A compound changes color but stays the same compound.

d. Two compounds change into other compounds.

6. A process in which substances undergo chemical change is called a(n) ______________________.

▶ Observing Chemical Reactions (pages 538–539)

7. Is the following sentence true or false? You can never detect a chemical reaction just by observing changes in properties of matter.

   ____

8. A solid that forms from solution during a chemical reaction is called a(n) ______________.

9. What is the key characteristic of a chemical reaction? ______________

   ____

   ____

   ____

10. Use *Exploring Evidence for Chemical Reactions* on page 539 to complete the table.

Evidence for Chemical Reactions	
Type of Evidence	**Observed Evidence**
	The color change of leaves in the fall
	A precipitate forms when solutions are mixed
	Oxygen bubbles form on the leaves of an underwater plant
	Water boils when placed on a natural-gas burner
	Soft dough changes into flaky bread in a hot oven

Name ______________________ Date __________ Class ______________

11. Are changes in properties always evidence for a chemical reaction?

Explain. ____

____

____

____

▶ Chemical Reactions on a Small Scale (pages 540–541)

12. Circle the letter of the sentence that is true about chemical reactions.

   a. Most chemical reactions involve only one step.

   b. A chemical reaction is a physical change of matter.

   c. Chemical reactions don't actually involve the particles of matter.

   d. A chemical reaction is the result of countless small changes.

13. How are chemical bonds involved in chemical reactions? ______________

____

____

14. Why is glass unreactive? ______________________________

____

____

SECTION 17-2 Describing Chemical Reactions (pages 544–551)

This section explains how to show chemical reactions with symbols. It also identifies three categories of chemical reactions.

▶ Introduction (page 544)

1. What is a chemical equation? ______________________________

____

____

▶ Writing Chemical Equations (pages 545–546)

2. Most elements are represented by a one-letter or two-letter

   ______________.

3. Use the table in Figure 6 on page 545 to write the symbol for each of the elements below.

   a. Phosphorus ____________ **b.** Aluminum ____________

   c. Chlorine ____________ **d.** Sodium ____________

   e. Iron ____________ **f.** Silver ____________

4. A combination of symbols that shows the ratio of elements in a compound is called a(n) ______________________.

5. Use the table in Figure 7 on page 545 to write the chemical formula for each of the compounds below.

   a. Ammonia ____________ **b.** Baking soda ____________

   c. Water ____________ **d.** Carbon dioxide ____________

   e. Sodium chloride ____________ **g.** Sugar ____________

6. What does a subscript show in a chemical formula? ______________

   ____

   ____

7. If a symbol in a chemical formula doesn't have a subscript, what is understood about that symbol? ______________________________

   ____

8. How many atoms of each kind of element are there in a molecule of carbon dioxide (CO_2)? ______________________________

   ____

   ____

Name ______________________ Date __________ Class ______________

9. The materials you have at the beginning of a chemical reaction are called ______________.

10. The materials you have when a chemical reaction is complete are called ______________.

11. What do you read the arrow in a chemical equation as meaning?

____

12. Label each chemical formula in the chemical equation below as either a reactant or a product.

$$Fe + S = FeS$$

______________ ______________ ______________

▶ Conservation of Mass (pages 546–547)

13. At the end of a chemical reaction, what is the total mass of the reactants compared to the total mass of the products? ______________

____

____

14. What is the principle called the conservation of mass? ______________

____

____

▶ Balancing Chemical Equations (pages 547–548)

15. A number in front of a chemical formula in a chemical equation is called a(n) ______________.

16. What does a coefficient tell you? ______________

____

____

17. Tell why this chemical equation is not balanced: $H_2 + O_2 = H_2O$.

____

____

____

18. Write the balanced equation for this reaction: Oxygen reacts with hydrogen to form water. ______________________

▶ Classifying Chemical Reactions (pages 549–551)

19. How can chemical reactions be classified? ______________________

____

____

20. Complete the table about the three categories of chemical reactions.

Categories of Chemical Reactions

Category	Description	Example Chemical Equation
	Two or more substances combine to make a more complex compound.	
	Compounds are broken down into simpler products.	
	One element replaces another in a compound, or two elements in different compounds trade places.	

21. Classify each of the following equations as synthesis, decomposition, or replacement.

a. $CaCO_3 \rightarrow CaO + CO_2$ ______________________

b. $2\ Na + Cl_2 \rightarrow 2\ NaCl$ ______________________

c. $Mg + CuSO_4 \rightarrow MgSO_4 + Cu$ ______________________

Name ________________ Date ________ Class ________

SECTION 17-3 Controlling Chemical Reactions
(pages 552–557)

This section explains how energy is related to chemical reactions. It also describes how the rate of a chemical reaction can be controlled.

▶ Energy in Chemical Reactions (page 553)

1. Is the following sentence true or false? Every chemical reaction involves a change of energy. ________________

2. A reaction that releases energy in the form of heat is called a(n) ________________.

3. A reaction that absorbs energy in the form of heat is called a(n) ________________.

4. On the graph below, how does the energy of the products compare with the energy of the reactants? ________________

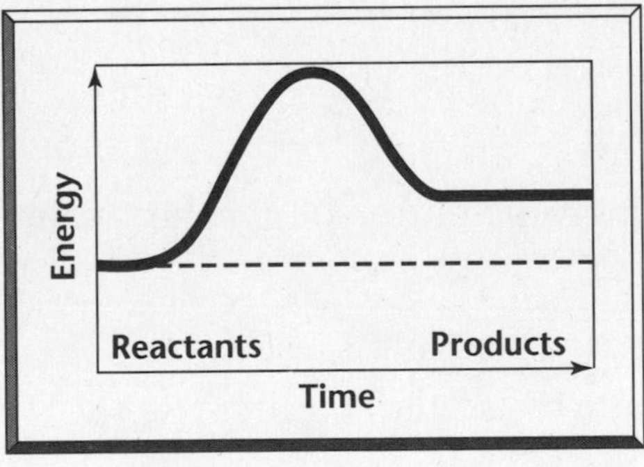

____

5. Label the graph above as either an exothermic or endothermic reaction.

▶ Getting Reactions Started (pages 553–554)

6. What is the activation energy of a chemical reaction? ________________

7. What part of the graph in question 4 above represents the activation energy for the reaction? ______________________

____

____

8. In a reaction that makes water from hydrogen and oxygen, where does the activation energy come from? ______________________

____

____

____

____

▶ Rates of Chemical Reactions (pages 554–557)

9. What are three factors that affect the rate of a chemical reaction?

a. ______________

b. ______________

c. ______________

10. The amount of one material in a given volume of another material is called ______________.

11. To increase the rate of a reaction, why would you increase the concentration of the reactants? ______________________

____

____

12. Circle the letter of each of the following that would increase the rate of a reaction.

a. Add heat.

b. Decrease the surface area.

c. Increase the surface area.

d. Reduce heat.

Name ______________________ Date __________ Class ______________

13. What is a catalyst? ____

____

____

14. Is the following sentence true or false? Catalysts are always permanently changed in a reaction. ______________

15. A biological catalyst is called a(n) ______________.

16. What is an inhibitor? ____

____

____

Reading Skill Practice

By looking carefully at illustrations in textbooks, you can help yourself understand better what you have read. Look carefully at Figure 16 on page 554. What important idea does this cartoon communicate? Do your work on a separate sheet of paper.

SECTION 17-4 Fire and Fire Safety
(pages 560-563)

This section describes the three things necessary to maintain a fire. It also explains how to prevent fires in the home.

▶ Understanding Fire (pages 560–562)

1. What is combustion? ____

____

____

____

2. A material that releases energy when it burns is called a(n)

_______________.

3. What are the three things necessary to start and maintain a fire?

a. ______________ b. ______________ c. ______________

4. Circle the letter of where the oxygen for a fire comes from.

a. air b. fuel c. reactants d. products

5. Is the following sentence true or false? An electric spark can provide the activation energy needed to start a combustion reaction. ______________

6. How does water remove two parts of the fire triangle? ______________

____

____

____

▶ Home Fire Safety (pages 562–563)

7. What are four common sources of fires?

a. ______________________

b. ______________________

c. ______________________

d. ______________________

8. Circle the letter of each way to fight a fire.

a. Blow air on it. b. Cover it with baking soda.

c. Use a fire extinguisher. d. Pour water on it.

9. Circle the letter of each of the following that is a safety aid in a fire-safe home.

a. smoke detectors b. gasoline can in the basement

c. fire extinguisher d. box of baking soda in the kitchen

Name ______________________ Date __________ Class ______________

WordWise

Complete the sentences by using one of the scrambled terms below.

Word Bank

mocpsoinoited	dcsutrop	emtrsyhc	msubocniot	ysisehtns
lmheiacc lmrauof	ntreactonionc	etaptiicrpe	tyltsaac	ctatsnaer
nioatvicat	rtiohbiin	eaeeplcmnrt		

1. A material that increases the rate of a reaction by lowering the activation energy is called a(n) ________________.
2. A chemical reaction that breaks down compounds into simpler products is called a(n) ________________ reaction.
3. A solid that forms from solution during a chemical reaction is called a(n) ________________.
4. The materials you have at the beginning of a chemical reaction are called ________________.
5. A chemical reaction in which two or more substances combine to make a more complex compound is called a(n) ________________ reaction.
6. The amount of one material in a given volume of another material is called ________________.
7. A material used to decrease the rate of a reaction is called a(n) ________________.
8. A rapid reaction between oxygen and a fuel is called ________________.
9. The minimum amount of energy that has to be added to start a chemical reaction is called the ________________ energy.
10. A chemical reaction in which one element replaces another in a compound, or in which two elements in different compounds trade places, is called a(n) ________________ reaction.
11. The substances formed as a result of a chemical reaction are called ________________.
12. A combination of symbols that shows the ratio of elements in a compound is called a(n) ________________.
13. The study of the properties of matter and how matter changes is called ________________.

Name ______________________ Date __________ Class ______________

MathWise

Balance the chemical equations below by adding coefficients. Write the balanced equations on the lines below.

▶ Balancing Chemical Equations (pages 547–549)

1. $H_2O \rightarrow H_2 + O_2$ ______________________

2. $N_2 + H_2 \rightarrow NH_3$ ______________________

3. $NH_3 \rightarrow N_2 + H_2$ ______________________

4. $K + H_2O \rightarrow H_2 + KOH$ ______________________

5. $Li + O_2 \rightarrow Li_2O$ ______________________

6. $Fe + O_2 \rightarrow Fe_2O_3$ ______________________

7. $Ag + N_2 \rightarrow Ag_3N$ ______________________

8. $C_2H_5OH + O_2 \rightarrow CO_2 + H_2O$ ______________________

Name ______________________ Date ________ Class ____________

CHAPTER 18

ATOMS AND BONDING

SECTION 18-1 Inside an Atom (pages 570–574)

This section describes the structure of an atom and explains the role that valence electrons play in forming chemical bonds.

▶ Structure of an Atom (pages 570–571)

1. What does an atom consist of? ______________________

____

____

Match the particle with its charge.

______ 2. neutron		**a.** positive
______ 3. proton		**b.** negative
______ 4. electron		**c.** neutral

5. Label the parts of an atom on the drawing.

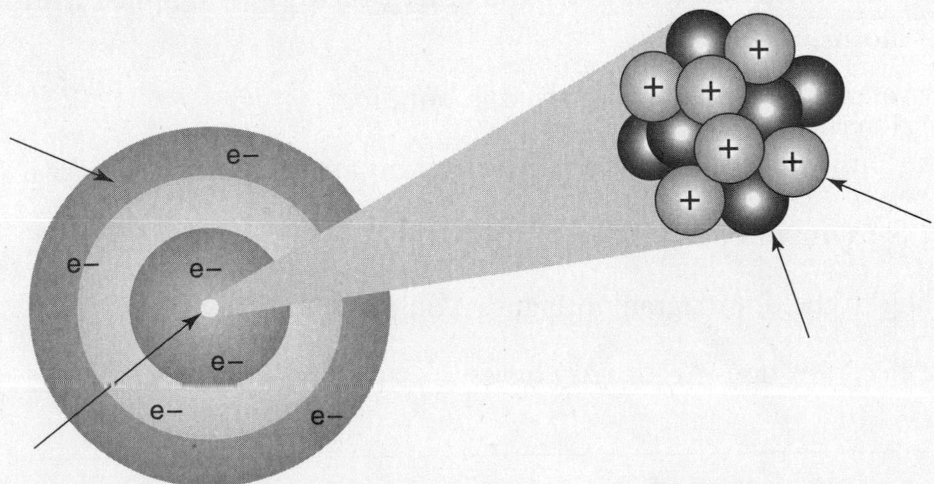

6. Circle the letter of each sentence that is true about the parts of an atom.
   - **a.** Protons are much lighter than electrons.
   - **b.** The number of neutrons always equals the number of protons in a nucleus.
   - **c.** In an atom, the number of protons equals the number of electrons.
   - **d.** Neutrons have about the same mass as electrons.

▶ Electrons in Atoms (pages 571–574)

7. Where does most of the mass of an atom come from? ______________________________

____

____

8. The space in which the electrons move is huge compared to the space occupied by the ______________.

9. What are the electrons farthest from the nucleus called?

____

10. Circle each sentence that is true about valence electrons.
    - **a.** The number of valence electrons an atom has determines whether or not the atom bonds with another atom.
    - **b.** The valence electrons are the only electrons in the electron cloud.
    - **c.** An atom's valence electrons help the other electrons form bonds with other atoms.
    - **d.** Only valence electrons are involved in bonding.

11. A way to show the number of valence electrons an atom has, using dots around the symbol of an element, is a(n) ______________________.

12. According to the dot diagram in Figure 3 on page 574, how many valence electrons does Argon (Ar) have? ______________________

____

▶ Why Atoms Form Bonds (page 574)

13. A chemical bond forms between two atoms when

_______________________ move between them.

14. What are two ways in which valence electrons move between atoms?

a. ____

____

b. ____

____

SECTION 18–2 Atoms in the Periodic Table (pages 575–577)

This section explains how the periodic table is organized. It also explains what the elements of each family have in common.

▶ Organizing the Elements (pages 575–576)

1. The number of protons in the nucleus of an atom is called the

_______________________.

2. How are the elements arranged in the periodic table? ______________

____

____

3. Complete the table by writing the definition of each term.

Organizing Elements	
Term	**Definition**
Group	
Family	
Period	

4. Is the following sentence true or false? The number of valence electrons increases from right to left across the periodic table. ______________

5. Are the elements represented in Figure 6 on page 576 from a row across the periodic table or a column down the periodic table? ______________

____

6. How many more valence electrons does a nitrogen atom have than a carbon atom? ______________

▶ Comparing Families of Elements (pages 576–577)

7. Circle the letter of the reason why each family in the periodic table has its own characteristic properties.

   a. Each element in a family has the same number of valence electrons.

   b. Each family shares its valence electrons among its elements.

   c. Each group has the same characteristics as a period.

   d. The periodic table begins with hydrogen.

8. Which group includes the noble gases? ______________

9. Why are the noble gases also known as inert gases? ______________

____

____

10. The elements of Group 17 are also called the ______________ gases.

11. Why does a fluorine atom react easily with other atoms that can give up electrons? ______________

____

____

12. Why are elements in the halogen family very reactive? ______________

____

Name ______________________ Date __________ Class ______________

13. What property makes the alkali metals very reactive? ______________

____

____

14. Is the following sentence true or false? Hydrogen is extremely reactive.

____

SECTION 18-3 Ionic Bonds (pages 579-584)

This section explains how an atom becomes electrically charged. It also describes the characteristic properties of bonds formed by the attraction of electrically charged atoms.

▶ Electron Transfer (pages 579–580)

1. An atom or group of atoms that has become electrically charged is a(n) ______________.

2. What happens to an atom when it loses an electron? ______________

____

____

3. What happens to an atom when it gains an electron? ______________

____

____

▶ Forming an Ionic Bond (pages 580–581)

4. What is an ionic bond? ______________

____

5. Why does a sodium atom become more stable when it loses one valence electron? ______________

____

6. What kind of ions do a sodium atom and a chlorine atom become when a valence electron is transferred from one to the other? ________

____

____

____

7. Use Figure 8 on page 580 to complete the table.

Ions and Their Charges		
Name	**Charge**	**Symbol or Formula**
Sodium		
Magnesium		
Chloride		
Sulfate		

8. What does the formula for the compound magnesium chloride, $MgCl_2$, tell you about how many chloride ions are needed to cancel out the charge of a magnesium ion? ____________________

____

____

▶ Polyatomic Ions (page 582)

9. Ions that are made of more than one atom are called

____________________.

10. How many atoms make up the carbonate ion (CO_3^{2-}), and what is its charge? ____________________

____

____

Name ______________________ Date __________ Class ______________

▶ Naming Ionic Compounds (page 582)

11. Is the following sentence true or false? In an ionic compound, the name of the negative ion comes first. ______________

12. When does the end of a name of a negative ion become *-ide*? ______________

____

▶ Properties of Ionic Compounds (pages 583–584)

13. What are three characteristic properties of ionic compounds?

a. ______________________

b. ______________________

c. ______________________

14. An orderly, three-dimensional arrangement formed by ions is called a(n) ______________.

15. In an ionic compound, every ion is attracted to what other ions? ______

____

____

16. At room temperature, ionic bonds are strong enough to cause all ionic compounds to be ______________.

17. When do ionic compounds conduct electricity well? ______________

____

Reading Skill Practice

A flowchart can help you remember the order in which events occur. On a separate sheet of paper, create a flowchart that describes the steps that take place when sodium and chlorine atoms form an ionic bond. This process is explained in *Exploring Ionic Bonds* on page 581. For more information about flowcharts, see page 833 in the Skills Handbook of your textbook.

Name ______________________ Date __________ Class ______________

SECTION 18-4

Covalent Bonds

(pages 585–589)

This section describes a chemical bond formed when two atoms share electrons. It also describes how electrons are shared unequally in some chemical bonds.

▶ Electron Sharing (page 585)

1. What is a covalent bond? ______________________________________

____

2. On the dot diagram below, draw a circle around the shared electrons that form a covalent bond between two fluorine atoms.

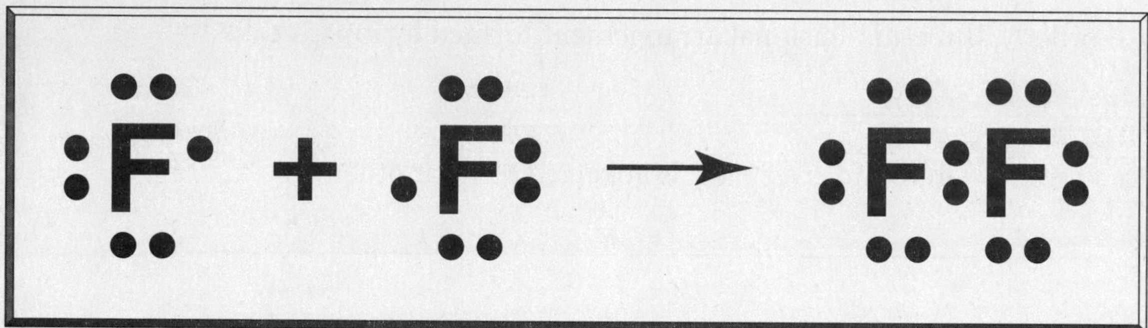

3. Circle the letter of the sentence that is true about a covalent bond in a molecule of fluorine.

a. Only the right atom attracts the two electrons in the middle.

b. Both atoms lose electrons.

c. Both atoms attract the two shared electrons at the same time.

d. Only the left atom attracts the two electrons in the middle.

▶ How Many Bonds? (page 586)

4. In the dot diagram of an oxygen molecule in Figure 13 on page 586, how many covalent bonds are in the molecule? ______________

5. A chemical bond formed when atoms share two pairs of electrons is called a(n) ______________________.

Name ______________________ Date __________ Class ______________

▶ Properties of Molecular Compounds (pages 586–587)

6. What do molecular compounds consist of? ______________________

____

____

7. Circle the letter of each sentence that is true about molecular compounds.

   a. More heat is needed to separate their molecules than is needed to separate ions.

   b. They melt at much lower temperatures than do ionic compounds.

   c. They boil at much lower temperatures than do ionic compounds.

   d. They are poor conductors of electricity.

▶ Unequal Sharing of Electrons (pages 587–588)

8. How do molecular compounds come to have a slight electrical charge?

____

____

____

____

9. In a polar covalent bond, electrons are shared ______________________.

10. How are electrons shared in a nonpolar covalent bond? ______________

____

____

11. How can a molecule be nonpolar even when it has polar bonds? ________

____

____

12. Is the following sentence true or false? Water molecules are polar.

____

Name ______________________ Date __________ Class ______________

CHAPTER 18, **Atoms and Bonding** *(continued)*

▶ Attractions Between Molecules (pages 588–589)

13. Why do polar and nonpolar molecules have different properties? ______

____

____

14. Why don't water and vegetable oil mix? ________________________

____

____

____

15. When you do laundry, what causes the nonpolar dirt to mix with the polar water? ____

____

SECTION 18–5 Crystal Chemistry (pages 592–594)

This section explains how chemical bonds are related to the properties of minerals.

▶ Mineral Properties (pages 592–593)

1. A naturally occurring solid that has a crystal structure and a definite chemical composition is called a(n) __________________.

2. What properties do mineralogists use to identify minerals? __________

____

____

3. What do all the properties of a mineral depend on? ______________

____

____

Name ______________________ Date __________ Class ______________

▶ Bonding in Mineral Crystals (pages 593–594)

4. Is the following sentence true or false? All mineral crystals are made of ions. ______________

5. What determines mineral properties such as crystal shape, hardness, and the way the crystal breaks apart? ______________________________

6. Complete the table about mineral crystals.

Mineral Crystals		
Type of Crystal	**How It Breaks**	**Example**
	Splits along face of like charges	
	Breaks apart into irregular shapes	

▶ Comparing Crystals (page 594)

7. Is the following sentence true or false? The stronger bonds of quartz make it harder than halite. ______________

8. If a mineralogist is in doubt about the identity of a mineral, what can he or she do? ______________________________

WordWise

Answer the questions by writing the correct key terms in the blanks. Use the numbered letters in the terms to find the hidden key term. Then write a definition for the hidden key term.

Clues	Key Terms
What particles form a cloud around the nucleus of an atom?	_ _ _ _ _ _ _ _ _ (4th blank: 1)
What is a covalent bond called in which electrons are shared unequally?	_ _ _ _ _ (2nd blank: 2)
______________ electrons are involved in bonding.	_ _ _ _ _ _ _ (1st blank: 3)
What is an orderly, three-dimensional arrangement formed by ions called?	_ _ _ _ _ _ _ (6th blank: 4)
What is the core of an atom?	_ _ _ _ _ _ _ (4th blank: 5, 5th blank: 6)
What is an atom or group of atoms that has become electrically charged?	_ _ _ (3rd blank: 7)
What is the neutral particle in an atomic nucleus?	_ _ _ _ _ _ _ (4th blank: 8)
What is the attraction between two oppositely charged ions called?	_ _ _ _ _ _ _ _ _ (1st blank of second word: 9)
What is a bond in which electrons are shared equally?	_ _ _ _ _ _ _ _ _ (5th blank: 10)
What is the positive particle in an atomic nucleus?	_ _ _ _ _ _ (6th blank: 11)
What is a bond in which two pairs of electrons are shared between atoms?	_ _ _ _ _ _ _ _ _ _ (1st blank: 12)

Key Term: _ _ _ _ _ _ _ _   _ _ _ _
1 2 3 4 5 6 7 8   9 10 11 12

Definition: ____

Name ______________________ Date __________ Class ______________

CHAPTER 19

Acids, Bases, and Solutions

SECTION 19-1

Working With Solutions
(pages 600–607)

This section explains what happens to particles of substances in solution. It also describes properties of solutions.

▶ Solutions and Suspensions (pages 600–601)

1. What is a suspension? ____

____

____

2. A well-mixed mixture is called a(n) ________________.

3. Circle the letter of the mixture that is evenly mixed throughout.

a. mixture **b.** solution **c.** suspension **d.** compound

4. Circle the letter of each method you could use to separate salt from water.

a. filtering **b.** boiling **c.** evaporation **d.** settling

▶ Solvents and Solutes (pages 601–602)

5. Complete the table about solvents and solutes.

Parts of a Solution		
Part	**Definition**	**Which Part of Salt Water Solution?**
	The part of a solution present in the largest amount	
	A substance present in a solution in a smaller amount	

6. In a solution, the ________________ is dissolved by the

________________.

7. Why is water called the "universal solvent"? ______________________

____

____

8. According to the table in Figure 3 on page 602, what is the solute and what is the solvent in the solution called air? ______________________

____

____

▶ Particles in a Solution (pages 602–603)

9. What happens to the solute's particles whenever a solution forms?

____

____

____

10. Circle the letter of each sentence that is true about particles in a solution.
    - a. When an ionic solid mixes with water, its ions repel water molecules.
    - b. When a molecular solid mixes with water, the covalent bonds are undisturbed.
    - c. When an ionic solid mixes with water, water molecules surround each ion.
    - d. When a molecular solid mixes with water, the solute's molecules break up.

▶ Concentration (page 603)

Match the term with its definition.

Term	Definition
______ 11. dilute solution	a. A mixture that has a lot of solute dissolved in it.
______ 12. concentrated solution	b. A mixture that has only a little solute dissolved in it.

▶ Solubility (page 604)

13. What is solubility? ______________________

____

14. A mixture that has so much solute in it that no more will dissolve is called a(n) ______________________.

15. A mixture in which more solute can be dissolved is called a(n) ______________________.

16. Which is more soluble in water, salt or sugar? ______________________

▶ Changing Solubility (pages 604–605)

17. What are two factors that affect the solubility of a substance?

a. ______________________ **b.** ______________________

18. Circle the letter of each sentence that is true about temperature and solubility.

a. Most solids become more soluble as the temperature goes up.

b. Most gases become less soluble as the temperature goes up.

c. Sugar dissolves better in cold water than in hot water.

d. Carbon dioxide dissolves better in cold water than in hot water.

19. Is the following sentence true or false? Ionic and polar compounds dissolve in polar solvents. ______________________

▶ Effects of Solutes on Solutions (pages 606–607)

20. Circle the letter of each sentence that is true about the effects of solutes on solutions.

a. Solutes raise the boiling point of a solvent.

b. The temperature must drop lower than 0°C for water to freeze when a solute is dissolved in the water.

c. Solutes raise the freezing point of a solvent.

d. Antifreeze boils at a lower temperature than pure water.

SECTION 19-2 Describing Acids and Bases (pages 610–615)

This section describes properties of compounds called acids and bases.

▶ Properties of Acids (pages 611–613)

1. What three properties are characteristic of an acid?

a. ______________________

b. ______________________

c. ______________________

2. If you were a scientist, why wouldn't you use "sour taste" to identify a compound as acidic? ______________________

____

____

3. Why are acids often identified as corrosive? ______________________

____

4. Complete the flowchart about etching.

An artist coats a(n) ______________________ with beeswax.

↓

The artist cuts a design in the ______________________, exposing the metal.

↓

When the plate is treated with a(n) ______________________, the design forms on the metal.

↓

Later, ______________________ applied to the plate collects in the grooves made by the acid.

Name ______________________ Date __________ Class ______________

5. What do carbonate ions contain? ______________________

____

6. What happens when acids react with compounds made of carbonates?

____

7. What kind of rock is made of calcium carbonate?

a. granite **b.** sandstone **c.** limestone **d.** coal

8. What happens when a dilute solution of hydrochloric acid is poured on a limestone rock? ______________________

9. Why would bubbles appear if an acid were poured on chalk? __________

____

10. A compound that changes color in the presence of an acid or a base is called a(n) ______________.

11. Why does lemon juice turn blue litmus paper red? ______________

____

____

12. Is the following sentence true or false? Many of the vitamins in the foods you eat are acids. ______________

13. Complete the table using information in Figure 13 on page 611 and in *Exploring Uses of Acids* on page 613.

Common Acids		
Acid	**Formula**	**Use**
Hydrochloric acid		
Nitric acid		
Sulfuric acid		
Phosphoric acid		

▶ Properties of Bases (pages 614–615)

14. What three properties are characteristic of a base?

a. ____

b. ____

c. ____

15. Why do your hands feel slippery when you rub soap on them under water?

____

16. Is the following sentence true or false? Even a strong base can't hurt you if you touch it. ______________

17. Is the following sentence true or false? A safe way to identify a base is to feel it. ______________

18. Remembering the letter *b* will help you remember that b______________ turn litmus paper b______________.

19. If a compound doesn't react with a metal or a carbonate, what do you know about that compound? ______________________

20. Complete the table using information in *Exploring Uses of Bases* on page 614 and in Figure 15 on page 615.

Common Bases

Base	Formula	Use
Sodium hydroxide		
Calcium hydroxide		
Magnesium hydroxide		
Ammonia		
Calcium oxide		

Name ______________________ Date __________ Class ______________

SECTION 19-3 Acids and Bases in Solution
(pages 616–621)

This section explains what kinds of ions acids and bases form in water. It also describes how the concentrations of ions are measured in a solution.

▶ Acids in Solution (pages 616–617)

1. What is a hydrogen ion (H^+)? ______________________________

____

____

2. What do acids in water separate into? ______________________________

____

3. Any substance that forms hydrogen ions (H^+) in water can be called a(n) ______________.

▶ Bases in Solution (page 617)

4. What is a hydroxide ion (OH^-)? ______________________________

____

____

5. Any substance that forms hydroxide ions (OH^-) in water can be called a(n) ______________.

▶ Strengths of Acids and Bases (page 618)

6. Circle the letter of each sentence that is true about the strength of acids and bases.

   a. Strong bases produce more OH^- ions than weak bases.

   b. Weak acids produce more OH^- ions than strong acids.

   c. Strong acids produce more H^+ ions than weak acids.

   d. Weak bases produce more H^+ ions than strong bases.

CHAPTER 19, Acids, Bases, and Solutions *(continued)*

7. Circle the letter of each strong acid or strong base.

a. ammonia **b.** sulfuric acid **c.** lye **d.** citric acid

8. Is the following sentence true or false? A strong acid is safe as long as it's in a dilute solution. ________________

▶ Measuring pH (pages 618–619)

9. What is the pH scale? ______________________________________

____

____

10. On the scale below, add labels to show the pH of these substances: milk, soap, water, vinegar, lemon, and ammonia.

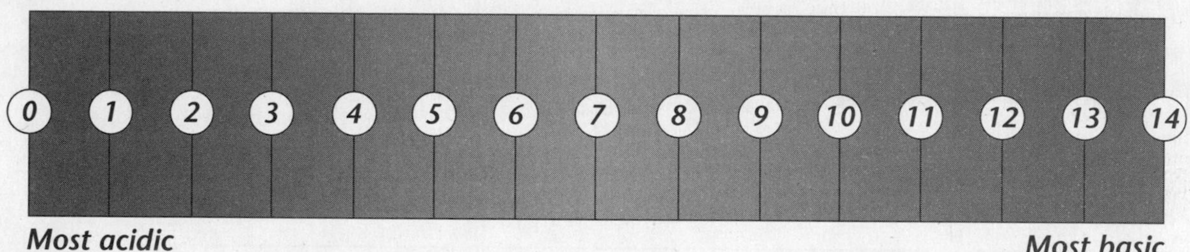

11. When the pH of a solution is low, is the concentration of hydrogen ions high or low? ________________

12. Circle the letter of each sentence that is true about pH.

a. A pH lower than 7 is acidic.

b. A pH of 7 is neutral.

c. A pH lower than 7 is basic.

d. A pH higher than 7 is acidic.

▶ Acid Rain (page 620)

13. Rain that is more acidic than normal rainwater is called

________________.

Name ______________________ Date __________ Class ______________

14. Why is acid rain a problem? ____

____

____

____

▶ Acid-Base Reactions (page 620)

15. A reaction between an acid and a base is called a(n)

______________________.

16. Is the following sentence true or false? An acid-base mixture is always more acidic than the starting solutions were. ______________

▶ Products of Acid-Base Reactions (page 621)

17. What is a salt? ____

____

____

18. What two substances does a neutralization reaction produce?

a. ______________

b. ______________

19. Circle the letter of the salt that is used as a de-icer for roads and walkways.

a. KCl b. ammonium nitrate c. $CaCO_3$ d. calcium chloride

Reading Skill Practice

When you read about complex topics, writing an outline can help you organize and understand the material. Outline Section 19–3 by using the headings and subheadings as topics and subtopics of your outline and then writing the most important details under each topic. Do your work on a separate sheet of paper.

SECTION 19-4

Digestion and pH

(pages 624–626)

This section explains why it is necessary for your body to digest food. It also explains how pH affects digestion.

▶ What Is Digestion? (pages 624–625)

1. The process that breaks down the complex molecules of food into smaller molecules is called ________________.

2. Why must foods be broken down in your body? ________________

____

____

____

3. Complete the table about the two processes of digestion.

Digestion	
Digestive Process	**Description**
Mechanical digestion	
Chemical digestion	

4. What biological catalysts help chemical digestion take place?

____

5. Circle the letter of each sentence that is true about digestive enzymes.

   a. Enzymes require just the right temperature and pH to work.

   b. The pH must be neutral for enzymes to work.

   c. Some enzymes require the pH to be high.

   d. Some enzymes require the pH to be low.

Name _______________ Date ________ Class ___________

▶ pH in the Digestive System (pages 625–626)

6. Is the following sentence true or false? The pH is not the same in all parts of the digestive system. _______________

7. What is amylase? _______________

8. Amylase works best when the pH is near _______________.

9. The stomach starts digestion of which kind of foods? _______________

10. What occurs in your stomach that drops the pH to a very acidic level of about 2? _______________

11. What does pepsin do? _______________

12. Pepsin works most effectively in _______________.

13. What does food move into when it leaves the stomach? _______________

14. Why does the pH in the small intestine rise to about 8? _______________

15. Is the following sentence true or false? Enzymes in the small intestine work best in a slightly basic solution. _______________

16. Most chemical digestion ends in the _______________.

WordWise

Match each definition in the left column with the correct term in the right column. Then write the number of each term in the appropriate box below. When you have filled in all the boxes, add up the numbers in each column, row, and two diagonals. All the sums should be the same.

A. A very well-mixed mixture

B. The part of a solution that is present in the smaller amount

C. A compound that changes color in the presence of an acid or a base

D. A substance that turns blue litmus paper red

E. A mixture that has a lot of solute dissolved in it

F. A negatively charged, polyatomic ion

G. A process that breaks down the complex molecules of food into smaller molecules

H. The part of a solution that is present in the larger amount

I. Any ionic compound that can form from the neutralization of an acid with a base

1. solute
2. digestion
3. hydroxide ion (OH^-)
4. salt
5. concentrated solution
6. solution
7. acid
8. indicator
9. solvent

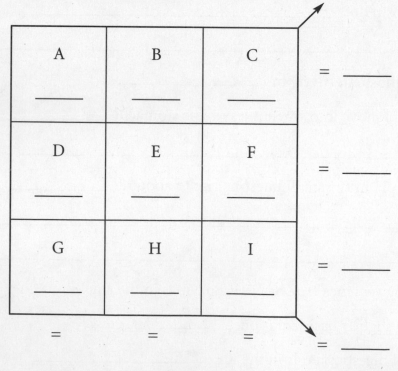

			↗ = _____
A _____	B _____	C _____	= _____
D _____	E _____	F _____	= _____
G _____	H _____	I _____	= _____
= _____	= _____	= _____	↘ = _____

Name ______________________ Date __________ Class ______________

CHAPTER 20

EXPLORING MATERIALS

SECTION 20-1 Polymers and Composites (pages 632–639)

This section explains how large, complex molecules form. It also describes properties of materials made of two or more substances.

▶ Carbon's Strings, Rings, and Other Things (page 633)

1. What do plastics and cells in your body have in common? ______________

____

____

2. Circle the letter of the number of covalent bonds that a carbon atom can form.

a. 2 **b.** 3 **c.** 4 **d.** 5

▶ Carbon Compounds Form Polymers (page 633)

3. A large, complex molecule built from smaller molecules joined together is a(n) ______________.

4. Describe three repeating patterns found in different polymers.

a. ____

____

b. ____

____

c. ____

____

Name ______________________ Date __________ Class ______________

5. The smaller molecules from which polymers are built are called

______________.

▶ Natural Polymers (page 634)

6. Is the following sentence true or false? Living things produce the polymers they need from materials in the environment. ______________

7. What is cellulose? ____

____

8. Is the following sentence true or false? Your best wool sweater is made from natural polymers. ______________

9. In your body, proteins are polymers made from monomers called

______________.

▶ Synthetic Polymers (page 635)

10. Complete the concept map about synthetic polymers.

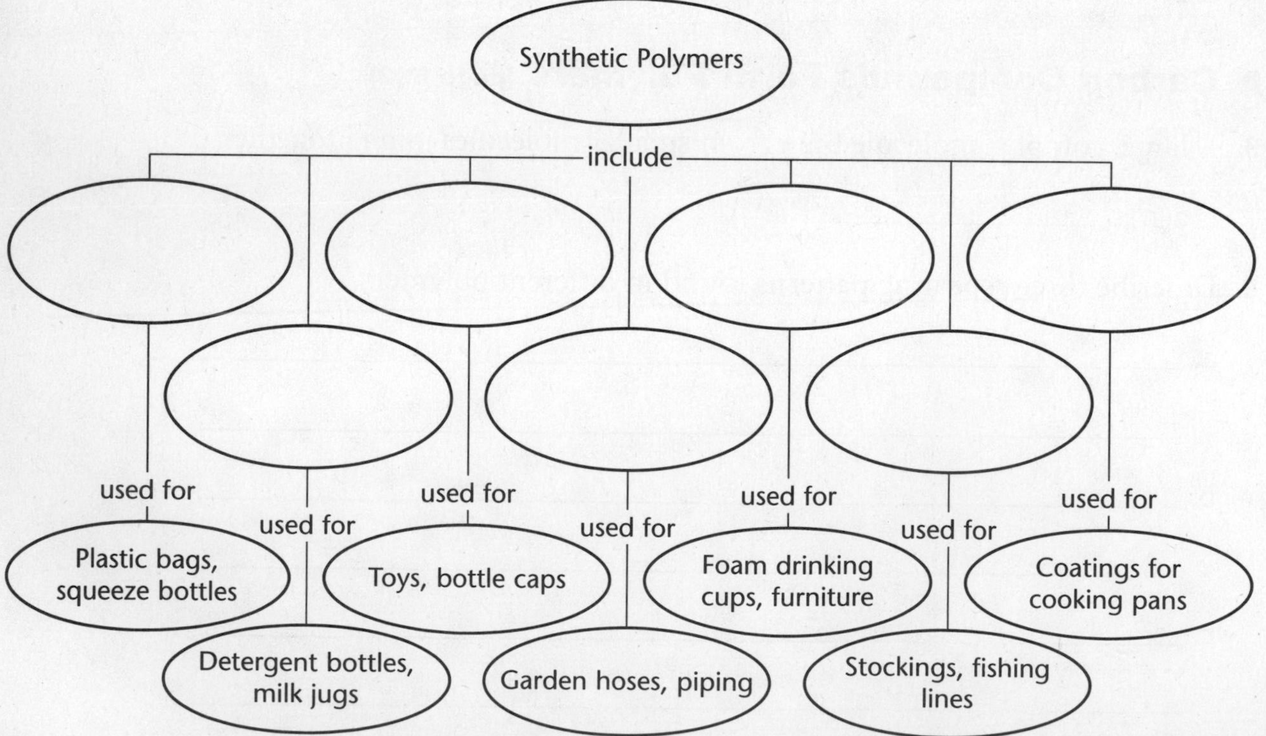

Name ______________________ Date __________ Class __________

11. The starting materials for most synthetic polymers come from

______________________.

12. What are plastics? ______________________

____

____

13. Why are synthetic polymers often used in place of some natural materials?

____

____

▶ Composites (pages 636–638)

14. What are composites? ______________________

____

____

15. Why do chemists make composite materials? ______________________

____

____

____

16. What are fiberglass composites composed of? ______________________

____

____

____

▶ Too Many Polymers? (pages 638–639)

17. What are two disadvantages of using plastics? ______________________

____

____

____

18. What is one solution to solve the problems of plastics? ______

______

______

______

Reading Skill Practice

Writing a summary can help you remember the information you have read. When you write a summary, write only the most important points. On a separate sheet of paper, write a summary of Section 20–1. Your summary should be shorter than the text on which it is based.

SECTION 20–2 Metals and Alloys
(pages 643–647)

This section describes the properties of metals and substances made of two or more elements that are like metals.

▶ Introduction (page 643)

1. What is an alloy? ______

______

______

▶ Properties of Metals (page 643)

2. What are three properties of metals?

a. ______

b. ______

c. ______

Name ______________________ Date __________ Class ______________

▶ Properties of Alloys (page 644)

3. How is bronze a better material than the elements that compose it?

____

____

4. Why are alloys used much more than pure metals? ______________

____

____

5. Is the following sentence true or false? Gold alloys are much harder than pure gold. ______________

6. To make an airplane's "skin" strong, what is alloyed with aluminum?

____

7. Airplane turbine blades are made of nickel alloyed with iron, carbon, and cobalt. What properties does that alloy have that make it able to do the job? ______________

____

____

▶ Making Alloys (page 644)

8. How have copper alloys been made since the beginning of the Bronze Age?

____

____

9. Circle the letter of two techniques used to make modern alloys.

a. Firing a beam of ions at a metal

b. Dipping the different elements in ice water

c. Mixing the elements as powders and then heating them under high pressure

d. Melting the metals and then spraying them onto another metal's surface

▶ Using Alloys (pages 645–647)

10. What properties does high-carbon steel have that make it more useful than wrought iron? ______________________________

____

11. Is the following sentence true or false? There are only three types of steel. ______________

12. What elements make up the alloy used to fill a cavity in a tooth?

____

13. Complete the Venn diagram to compare two types of steel.

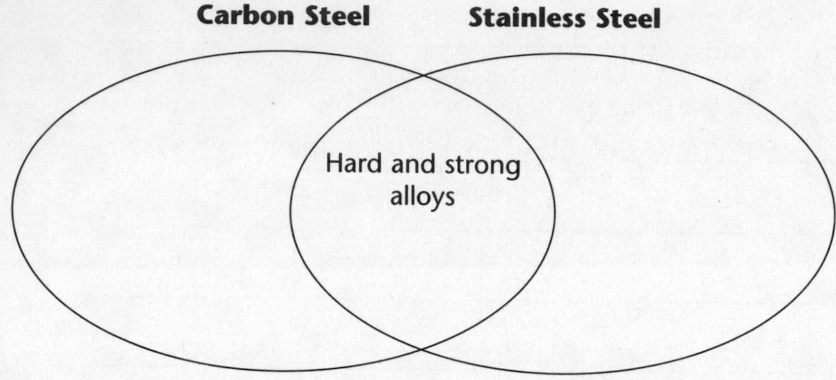

Match the alloy with the elements that make it up.

Alloy	Elements
____ 14. pewter	a. Iron, carbon, nickel, chromium
____ 15. brass	b. Tin, antimony, copper
____ 16. sterling silver	c. Copper, zinc
____ 17. stainless steel	d. Iron, carbon
____ 18. carbon steel	e. Silver, copper

19. What property does plumber's solder have that makes it useful for sealing joints and leaks in metal plumbing? ______________

____

Name ______________________ Date __________ Class ______________

SECTION 20-3

Ceramics and Glass
(pages 648–652)

This section describes the properties of solids made by heating clay and other minerals. It also explains how glass is made and used.

▶ Making Ceramics (pages 648–649)

1. Hard, crystalline solids made by heating clay and other materials to high temperatures are called ______________.

2. How does a potter get the water out of clay used to make ceramic pottery?

____

____

____

3. How does adding a glaze to a piece of pottery change the properties of the piece? ____

____

▶ Properties and Uses of Ceramics (pages 649–650)

4. Circle the letter of each property that makes ceramics useful.
   a. Ceramics do not conduct electricity.
   b. Ceramics resist moisture.
   c. Ceramics are brittle and can shatter when struck.
   d. Ceramics can withstand temperatures higher than those of molten metals.

5. Why are ceramic tiles used on the bottom of space shuttles?
   a. They withstand high temperatures.
   b. They protect against asteroids.
   c. They keep the shuttle waterproof.
   d. They let oxygen into the shuttle.

CHAPTER 20, Exploring Materials *(continued)*

6. What are three long-standing uses of ceramics?

a. ______________ **b.** ______________ **c.** ______________

▶ Making Glass (pages 650–651)

7. What is a clear, solid material with no crystal structure, created by heating sand to a very high temperature? ______________.

8. Why did early glassmakers add limestone and sodium carbonate to melting sand? ______________

____

▶ Communications Through Glass (pages 651–652)

9. What is an optical fiber? ______________

____

____

10. Circle the letter of each material that optical fiber is replacing.

a. telephone lines

b. ceramic pipelines

c. ceramic tiles

d. cable television lines

SECTION 20-4 Radioactive Elements (pages 653–659)

This section explains how radioactive elements change over time and describes how radioactive materials are used.

▶ Nuclear Reactions (page 654)

1. Why can't one element be made into another element by a chemical reaction? ______________

____

Name ______________________ Date __________ Class ______________

2. What are nuclear reactions? ______________________

____

▶ Isotopes (page 654)

3. Atoms with the same number of protons and different numbers of neutrons are called ______________.

4. What is the mass number of an isotope? ______________________

____

____

5. What is the mass number of carbon-12? ______________

6. Circle the letter of the correct number of protons and neutrons that an atom of carbon-14 has.

   a. 7 protons and 7 neutrons

   b. 14 protons and 14 neutrons

   c. 6 protons and 8 neutrons

   d. 8 protons and 6 neutrons

▶ Radioactive Decay (pages 654–655)

7. Is the following sentence true or false? The nucleus of an unstable atom does not hold together well. ______________

8. What happens in the process called radioactive decay? ______________

____

____

9. The particles and energy produced during radioactive decay are forms of ______________________.

10. Circle the letter of the type of nuclear radiation that is most penetrating.

    a. alpha particle **b.** beta particle **c.** gamma radiation **d.** isotope

CHAPTER 20, Exploring Materials *(continued)*

11. Complete the table about radioactive decay.

Radioactive Decay		
Type of Radiation	**Description**	**Type of Radioactive Decay**
Alpha particle		
Beta particle		
Gamma radiation		

12. Label each illustration below according to which type of radioactive decay it represents.

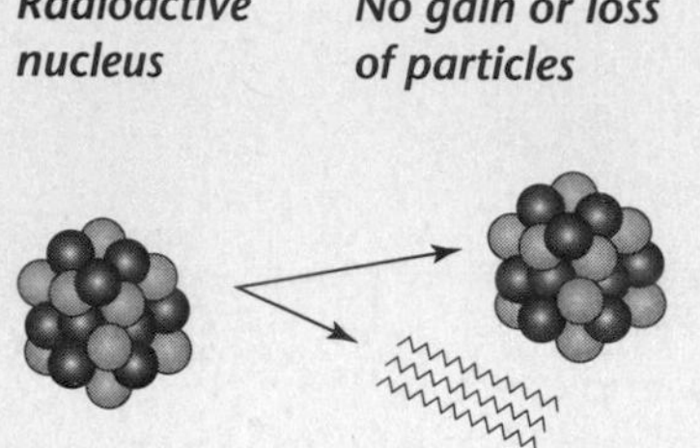

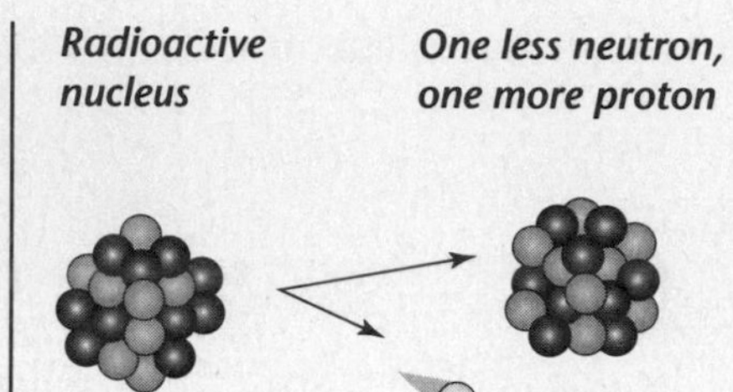

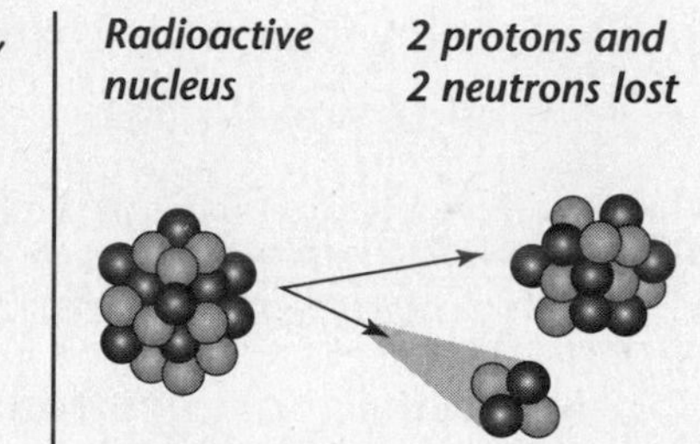

______________ ______________ ______________

▶ Half-Life (page 656)

13. What is the half-life of an isotope? ______________________________

____

____

14. Rank the following isotopes according to the length of their half-lives. Rank the isotope with the longest half-life as *1*.

_____ iodine-131

_____ carbon-14

_____ uranium-238

_____ cobalt-60

15. The process of determining the age of an object using the half-life of one or more radioactive isotopes is called ______________________.

▶ Using Radioactive Isotopes (pages 657–658)

16. What are tracers? ______________________

____

____

17. How can biologists learn where and how plants use phosphorus? ______

____

____

____

18. How were the images made that are shown in Figure 24 on page 658?

____

____

____

____

19. The process in which radioactive elements are used to destroy unhealthy cells is called ______________________.

20. What do nuclear power plants most often use as fuel?

____

▶ Safe Use of Radioactive Materials (page 659)

21. How will dangerous radioactive materials be disposed of in the future?

____

____

____

Name ______________________ Date __________ Class ______________

WordWise

Solve the clues by filling in the blanks with key terms from Chapter 20. Then write the numbered letters in the correct order to find the hidden message.

Clues	Key Terms
A solid material with no crystal structure	_ _ _ _ _ (4th blank: 1)
Synthetic polymers that can be molded and shaped	_ _ _ _ _ _ _ _ (5th blank: 2)
A natural polymer that gives shape to plant cells	_ _ _ _ _ _ _ _ _ (2nd blank: 3; 9th blank: 4)
The time needed for half the atoms of an isotope sample to decay	_ _ _ _ - _ _ _ _ (5th blank: 5)
Hard, crystalline solids made by heating clay and other materials	_ _ _ _ _ _ _ _ (6th blank: 6)
A combination of two or more substances that creates a new material	_ _ _ _ _ _ _ _ _ (6th blank: 7)
A ________ reaction involves the particles in the nucleus of an atom.	_ _ _ _ _ _ _ (6th blank: 8)
Small, carbon-based molecules	_ _ _ _ _ _ _ _ (3rd blank: 9)
A radioactive isotope that can be followed through the steps of a chemical reaction	_ _ _ _ _ _ (3rd blank: 10)
A large, complex, carbon-based molecule	_ _ _ _ _ _ _ (3rd blank: 11)
The particles and energy produced during radioactive decay	_ _ _ _ _ _ _ (4th blank: 12)
A process in which atomic nuclei of unstable isotopes release fast-moving particles and energy	_ _ _ _ _ _ _ _ _ (8th blank: 13) _ _ _ _ _ _ _ _ _ _ _ _ _ _ (4th blank: 14)

Hidden Message

_ _ _ _ _   _ _   _ _   _ _ _ _ _.

1 2 3 4 5   6 7   8 9   10 11 12 13 14

Name ______________________ Date __________ Class __________

CHAPTER 21

Chemistry of Living Systems

SECTION 21-1 Chemical Bonding, Carbon Style (pages 666–669)

This section explains why carbon can form a huge variety of different compounds. It also describes the different forms of pure carbon.

▶ The Carbon Atom and Its Bonds (page 667)

1. Circle the letter of the number of valence electrons a carbon atom has available for bonding.

   a. 2 **b.** 4 **c.** 6 **d.** 8

2. The transfer or sharing of valence electrons creates chemical

   __________________.

3. Is the following sentence true or false? Carbon atoms form more bonds than most other atoms. __________________

4. Circle the letter of the number of bonds each carbon atom is able to form.

   a. 2 **b.** 4 **c.** 6 **d.** 8

5. What are three ways carbon atoms bond to form the backbones for molecules?

   a. ______________ **b.** ______________ **c.** ______________

▶ Forms of Pure Carbon (pages 668–669)

6. Why can the pure element of carbon exist in different forms? __________

   ____

   ____

7. Complete the table about forms of pure carbon.

Forms of Carbon			
Form	**Arrangement of Carbon Atoms**	**Properties**	**Use**
Diamond			
		Soft, slippery	Pencils, lubricants
	Ball-shaped repeating pattern	Enclose an open area	Possibly hold medicine or computer circuits

8. Under what conditions do diamonds form? ______________________________

____

____

9. How did fullerenes get their name? ______________________________

____

SECTION 21–2 Carbon Compounds
(pages 671–678)

This section describes the properties that many carbon compounds have in common. It also describes carbon compounds that contain only the elements carbon and hydrogen.

▶ Organic Compounds (pages 671–672)

1. Most compounds that contain carbon are called ______________________

______________________.

2. Why are many organic compounds liquid or gas at room temperature?

____

____

3. Circle the letter of each sentence that is true about organic compounds.

   a. They generally have strong odors.

   b. They have high boiling points.

   c. Many don't dissolve well in water.

   d. They are good conductors of electric currents.

▶ Hydrocarbons (pages 672–673)

4. What is a hydrocarbon? ______________________________________

   ____

5. What are three carbon chains that form in hydrocarbons?

   a. ______________ b. ______________ c. ______________

6. Why are hydrocarbons used for fuel in stoves, cars, and airplanes?

   ____

   ____

7. A number in a molecular formula that tells you the number of atoms of an element in a compound is called a(n) ______________.

8. This is the molecular formula for a hydrocarbon called propane: C_3H_8.

   What does this formula tell you about a molecule of propane? ________

   ____

   ____

▶ Straight Chains and Branches (page 674)

9. What does a structural formula show about a molecule of a compound?

   ____

   ____

10. Each dash in a structural formula represents a chemical

    ______________.

11. The partially complete structural formula below shows the "backbone" for a propane molecule. Complete the structural formula of this hydrocarbon by showing all the hydrogen atoms that are bonded to the carbon chain.

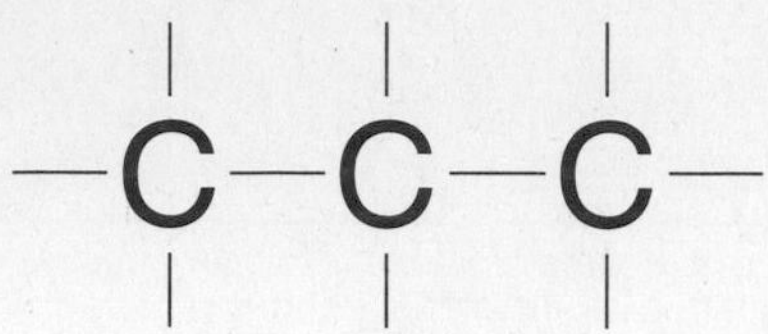

Propane (C_3H_8)

12. Compounds that have the same molecular formula but different structures are called _______________.

▶ Double Bonds and Triple Bonds (page 675)

13. How do structural formulas represent a double bond in a molecule?

____

▶ Saturated and Unsaturated Hydrocarbons (page 675)

14. Complete the table about saturated and unsaturated hydrocarbons.

Saturated and Unsaturated Hydrocarbons			
Type of Hydrocarbon	**Bonds**	**Ending on Names**	**Example**
	Single bonds		Ethane
	Double or triple bonds	*-ene* or *-yne*	

▶ Substituted Hydrocarbons (pages 676–677)

15. A hydrocarbon in which one or more hydrogen atoms have been replaced by atoms of other elements is called a(n)

_______________.

16. In compounds that contain halogens, what replaces hydrogen atoms?

____

____

17. Circle the letter of the hydroxyl group.

a. –HO **b.** –COOH **c.** –OH **d.** –COH

18. A substituted hydrocarbon that contains one or more hydroxyl groups is called a(n) ______________.

19. Circle the letter of each alcohol.

a. freon **b.** ethane **c.** acetic acid **d.** methanol

20. Circle the letter of the carboxyl group.

a. –HO **b.** –COOH **c.** –OH **d.** –COH

21. A substituted hydrocarbon that contains one or more carboxyl groups is called a(n) ______________.

▶ Esters (page 677)

22. An organic compound made by chemically combining an alcohol and an organic acid is called a(n) ______________.

▶ Polymers (page 678)

23. What is a polymer? ____

____

____

24. The smaller molecules that make up polymers are called ______________.

25. What are synthetic polymers? ____

____

____

Reading Skill Practice

By looking carefully at illustrations in textbooks, you can help yourself better understand what you have read. Look carefully at Figure 11 on page 674. What important idea does this figure communicate?

SECTION 21-3 Life With Carbon

(pages 679–687)

This section describes the four main classes of polymers in living things.

▶ Nutrients From Foods (page 680)

1. Substances that provide the energy and raw materials the body needs to grow, repair worn parts, and function properly are called

   ________________.

2. The process of breaking apart large molecules into small molecules is called ________________.

3. What are the four classes of polymers found in all living things?

   a. ________________ b. ________________

   c. ________________ d. ________________

▶ Carbohydrates (pages 680–682)

4. What is a carbohydrate? ________________

   ____

   ____

5. Circle the letter of the simplest carbohydrates.

   a. proteins b. esters c. sugars d. hydrocarbons

6. The sugar with the molecular formula of $C_6H_{12}O_6$ is called

______________.

7. Why is glucose sometimes called "blood sugar"? ______________

____

____

8. A long chain of simple carbohydrates is called a(n) ______________

______________.

9. Complete the table about complex carbohydrates.

Complex Carbohydrates		
Type	**Description**	**Contained in These Foods**
Starch		
Cellulose		

▶ Proteins (pages 682–683)

10. Polymers made of organic compounds called amino acids are

______________.

11. Is the following sentence true or false? There are four different kinds of amino acids. ______________

12. What elements make up amino acids? ______________

____

____

13. Circle the letter of each food that is a good source of protein.

a. fish **b.** beans **c.** potatoes **d.** meat

14. What does the body use proteins for? ______________________________

____

▶ Lipids (pages 684–685)

15. What are lipids? ______________________________

____

16. What are four types of lipids?

a. ______________ b. ______________

c. ______________ d. ______________

17. Gram for gram, which stores more energy, lipids or carbohydrates?

____

18. What is each fat or oil molecule made of? ______________________________

____

____

19. A waxy lipid found in all animal cells is called ______________.

▶ Nucleic Acids (page 686)

20. What are nucleic acids? ______________________________

____

____

21. Complete the table about types of nucleic acids.

Nucleic Acids		
Common Name	**Full Name**	**Composed of**
	Deoxyribonucleic acid	Four kinds of
	Ribonucleic acid	Four kinds of

22. The monomers that make up nucleic acids are called

______________.

23. What do the differences among living things depend on? ______________

____

____

24. Complete the flowchart about nucleic acids.

The order of nucleotides in ______________ determines

↓

the order of nucleotides in ______________, which determines

↓

the order of ______________ in proteins.

▶ Other Nutrients in Foods (page 687)

25. Complete the table about other nutrients in foods.

Vitamins and Minerals		
Nutrient	**Definition**	**Examples**
Vitamins		
Minerals		

26. Is the following sentence true or false? You will probably get the vitamins and minerals you need if you eat a variety of foods.

____

WordWise

Use the clues below to identify key terms from Chapter 21. Write the terms on the lines, putting one letter in each blank. When you finish, the word enclosed in the diagonal will reveal an important term related to the chemistry of living things. Define the term.

Clues

1. Substances that provide the energy and raw materials for the body
2. A form of pure carbon with atoms arranged in a ball-shaped repeating pattern
3. A substituted hydrocarbon that contains one or more hydroxyl groups
4. A sugar found in the body
5. Elements needed by your body
6. A –COOH group found in organic acids
7. A formula that shows the kind, number, and arrangement of atoms in a molecule
8. The monomers in a protein molecule
9. A compound that contains only the elements carbon and hydrogen
10. An organic compound made by chemically combining an alcohol and an organic acid

1. _ _ _ _ _ _ _ _ _
2. _ _ _ _ _ _ _ _ _
3. _ _ _ _ _ _ _
4. _ _ _ _ _ _ _
5. _ _ _ _ _ _ _ _
6. _ _ _ _ _ _ _ _ _ _ _ _ _
7. _ _ _ _ _ _ _ _ _ _ _ _ _ _ _ _ _
8. _ _ _ _ _ _ _ _ _ _
9. _ _ _ _ _ _ _ _ _ _ _
10. _ _ _ _ _

Definition: ____

____

Name ______________________ Date __________ Class ______________

CHAPTER 22

EARTH, MOON, AND SUN

SECTION 22-1 Earth in Space

(pages 704–711)

This section explains what causes day and night and what causes the cycle of seasons on Earth.

▶ Days and Years (pages 705–707)

1. The study of the moon, stars, and other objects in space is called

_______________.

Match the term with its definition.

	Term	Definition
______	**2.** axis	**a.** The movement of one object around another object
______	**3.** rotation	**b.** The imaginary line that passes through Earth's center and the North and South poles
______	**4.** revolution	**c.** The path of an object as it revolves around another object in space
______	**5.** orbit	**d.** The spinning motion of a planet around its axis

6. Each 24-hour cycle of day and night is called a(n) _______________.

7. Why is an extra day added to February every four years? __________

____

____

____

____

8. What causes day and night? ____

____

▶ Seasons on Earth (pages 708–711)

9. Why is it warmer near the equator than near the poles? ____________

____

____

____

10. Why does Earth have seasons? ____

____

____

11. Circle the letter of each sentence that is true when the Northern Hemisphere has summer.

    a. The Southern Hemisphere is tilted away from the sun.

    b. The Northern Hemisphere is tilted away from the sun.

    c. The Southern Hemisphere is tilted toward the sun.

    d. The Northern Hemisphere is tilted toward the sun.

12. What is latitude? ____

____

____

13. Circle the letter of each sentence that is true about Earth's seasons.

    a. Earth is closest to the sun when it is summer in the Northern Hemisphere.

    b. The hemisphere that is tilted away from the sun has more daylight than the other hemisphere.

    c. When it is summer in the Northern Hemisphere it is winter in the Southern Hemisphere.

    d. In December, the sun's rays in the Northern Hemisphere are indirect.

Name ______________________ Date __________ Class ______________

14. Each of the two days of the year when the sun is overhead at either 23.5° south or 23.5° north is called a(n) ________________.

15. Each of the two days of the year when neither hemisphere is tilted toward or away from the sun is called a(n) ________________.

16. Complete the table.

Earth's Seasons			
Day in Northern Hemisphere	**Approximate Date Each Year**	**Length of Daytime**	**Which Hemisphere Is Tilted Toward the Sun?**
Summer solstice			
Autumnal equinox			
Winter solstice			
Vernal equinox			

SECTION 22-2 Phases, Eclipses, and Tides (pages 714–724)

This section explains what causes phases of the moon, what causes eclipses, and what causes the tides.

▶ Introduction (page 714)

1. What causes the phases of the moon, eclipses, and tides? ________________

____

▶ Motions of the Moon (pages 714–715)

2. Circle the letter of each sentence that is true about motions of the moon.

   a. The moon revolves around the Earth once a year.

   b. The "near side" of the moon always faces Earth.

   c. The moon rotates slowly on its axis once every 27.3 days.

   d. The moon's orbit around Earth is an oval shape.

▶ Phases of the Moon (pages 715–717)

3. The different shapes of the moon you see from Earth are called

_______________.

4. How often does the moon go through a whole set of phases? __________

____

____

____

5. What does the phase of the moon you see depend on? __________

____

____

6. Complete the table about phases of the moon.

Phases of the Moon	
Phase	**What You See**
New moon	
First quarter	
Full moon	
Third quarter	

▶ Eclipses (page 717)

7. When the moon's shadow hits Earth or Earth's shadow hits the moon,

what occurs? ______________________________________

8. What are the two types of eclipses?

a. ____________________ b. ____________________

▶ Solar Eclipses (page 718)

9. The darkest part of a shadow is called the _______________.

10. What happens to cause a solar eclipse? ______________________

____

____

11. The larger part of a shadow, surrounding the umbra, is called the

________________.

12. Circle the letter of each sentence that is true about solar eclipses.

a. People in the umbra see only a partial solar eclipse.

b. During a partial solar eclipse, part of the sun remains visible.

c. During a total solar eclipse, the sky is dark.

d. People in the penumbra see a total solar eclipse.

▶ Lunar Eclipses (page 719)

13. What is the arrangement of Earth, moon, and sun during a lunar eclipse? ______________________________________

____

14. Circle the letter of each sentence that is true about lunar eclipses.

a. People in Earth's umbra see a total lunar eclipse.

b. A lunar eclipse occurs at a full moon.

c. During a lunar eclipse, Earth blocks sunlight from reaching the moon.

d. A partial lunar eclipse occurs when the moon passes partly into the umbra of Earth's shadow.

▶ Tides (pages 722–724)

15. The rise and fall of the level of the ocean are called ________________.

16. What force pulls the moon and Earth toward each other?

____

17. Why do tides occur? ______________________________

____

____

CHAPTER 22, Earth, Moon, and Sun *(continued)*

18. Circle the letter of each sentence that is true about tides.

    a. The point on Earth that is closest to the moon has a high tide.

    b. Every location on Earth has two high tides per month.

    c. A low tide occurs at the point on Earth farthest from the moon.

    d. The water left behind at the point on Earth farthest from the moon has a high tide.

19. What is a spring tide? ____

    ____

20. What is a neap tide? ____

    ____

21. On each of the illustrations below, draw a moon to show its position at a spring tide and at a neap tide.

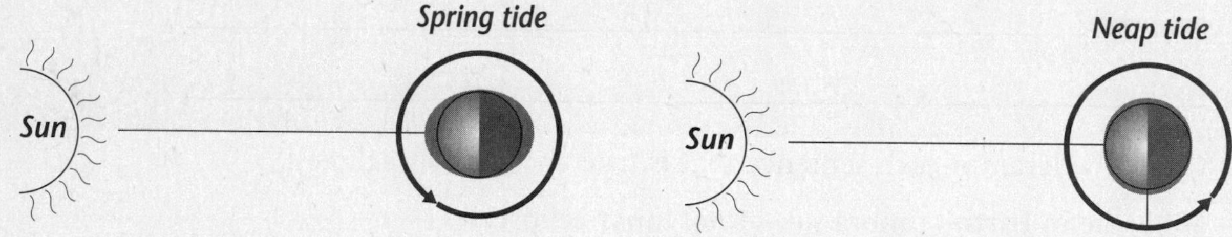

22. Circle the letter of each of the phases of the moon when a spring tide occurs.

    a. new moon   b. first quarter   c. full moon   d. third quarter

23. Is the following sentence true or false? Sometimes the effects of ocean tides extend far up rivers. ______________

Reading Skill Practice

By looking carefully at illustrations in textbooks, you can help yourself understand better what you have read. Look carefully at Figure 6 on page 717. What important idea does this figure communicate?

SECTION 22-3

Rockets and Satellites
(pages 725–728)

This section explains how rockets travel in space and describes what satellites and space stations are used for.

▶ How Rockets Work (page 725)

1. Why does a rocket move forward? ______________________________

____

____

2. For every force, or action, there is an equal and opposite force, or

________________.

▶ Multistage Rockets (page 726)

3. How many stages do multistage rockets have? ________________

4. What happens to each stage when it uses up its fuel? ______________

____

____

5. What did the development of multistage rockets make possible? _______

____

____

____

▶ Artificial Satellites (pages 726–727)

6. What is a satellite? ______________________________

____

____

7. Circle the letter of the first artificial satellite launched into space.

a. *Skylab* b. *Explorer 1* c. *Sputnik 1* d. *Mir*

8. What are four uses of satellites and space stations?

a. ______________ b. ______________

c. ______________ d. ______________

9. What does it mean when a satellite is in a geosynchronous orbit? ______

____

____

10. Circle the letter of each sentence that is true about geosynchronous orbits.

a. They seem to hover over a given point on Earth.

b. People can live on them for long periods.

c. They are used to map weather patterns.

d. People can find them on Earth's surface.

11. A large satellite in which people can live for long periods is called a(n)

______________.

12. What are the United States, Russia, and many other countries cooperating to build in space? ______________

▶ Space Shuttles (page 728)

13. Why are space shuttles called "shuttles"? ______________

____

14. What would be the ideal vehicle to launch people and cargo into space?

____

____

____

15. Is the following sentence true or false? Since 1981, space shuttles have been the main way that the United States launches astronauts and equipment into space. ______________

Name ______________________ Date __________ Class ______________

SECTION **22-4**

Earth's Moon

(pages 729–734)

This section describes the features of the moon that can be seen with a telescope. It also describes the missions to the moon.

▶ The Structure and Origin of the Moon (page 730)

1. Circle the letter of the approximate size of the moon.
   a. about twice the size of Earth
   b. about half Earth's diameter
   c. about the size of Hawaii
   d. about one quarter Earth's diameter

2. Complete the flowchart about the collision theory of the moon's origin.

A Theory of the Moon's Origin

A large object strikes ______________.

↓

Material from ______________ outer layer breaks off.

↓

The material from Earth is thrown into ______________.

↓

Material in orbit forms the ______________.

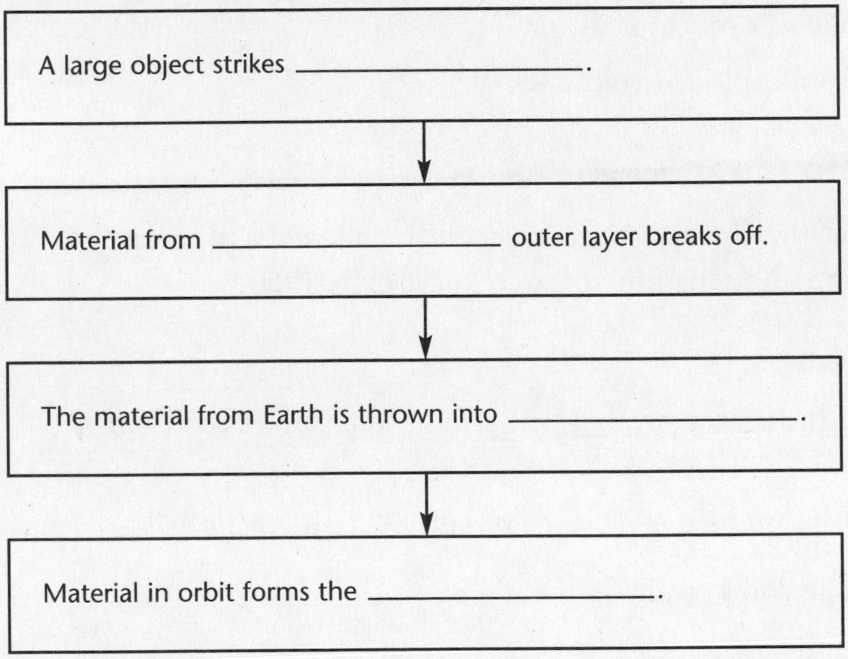

▶ Looking at the Moon From Earth (pages 730–731)

3. Who made a telescope in 1609 that allowed him to see details of the moon nobody had ever seen before? ______________________

____

4. Name three features on the moon's surface.

a. ______________________

b. ______________________

c. ______________________

5. Round pits on the surface of the moon are called ______________.

6. What are craters on the moon caused by? ______________________

____

____

7. Circle the letter of the phrase that best describes maria.

a. Highland peaks that cast dark shadows

b. Low, dry areas that were once flooded with molten material

c. Vast oceans that cover much of the moon

d. Craters made from exploded volcanoes

▶ Missions to the Moon (pages 732–734)

8. Which president of the United States launched an enormous program of space exploration and scientific research in the early 1960s?

____

9. Circle the letter of the spacecraft that flew into orbit around the moon in July, 1969.

a. *Surveyor* **b.** *Sputnik 1* **c.** *Skylab* **d.** *Apollo 11*

10. Who was the first person to walk on the moon? ______________

____

11. What did Neil Armstrong say when he took his first step onto the moon?

____

____

12. How have scientists learned about the material that makes up the moon's surface? ______________________

____

____

13. How do scientists know that the moon's surface once was very hot?

____

____

____

14. What did scientists conclude from moon rocks that had been broken apart and then reformed? ______________________

____

____

15. Is the following sentence true or false? The interior of the moon remains very hot. ______________

16. Is the following sentence true or false? Seismometers detected extremely strong moonquakes on the moon. ______________

17. Circle the letter of each sentence that is true about the far side of the moon.

a. It is almost completely covered with maria.

b. It is rougher than the near side.

c. It has few maria.

d. It is very smooth with no visible craters.

18. In 1998, what did the *Lunar Prospector* discover about the moon's poles?

____

____

____

Name ______________________ Date __________ Class ______________

WordWise

The hidden-word puzzle below contains 12 key terms from Chapter 22. You might find them across, down, or on the diagonal. Use the clues to identify the hidden terms. Then circle each term in the puzzle.

Clues	Key Terms
The spinning motion of a planet around its axis	____________
The study of the moon, stars, and other objects in space	____________
The shapes of the moon you see from Earth	____________
The imaginary line that passes through Earth's center and the North and South poles	____________
The two days of the year on which the sun is directly overhead at either 23.5° north or south	____________
Earth's path as it revolves around the sun	____________
The movement of one object around another object	____________
The rise or fall of the level of water in the ocean	____________
A round pit on the moon's surface	____________
The darkest part of a shadow	____________
Dark, flat areas on the moon's surface	____________
The part of a shadow that surrounds the darkest part	____________

x c r a t e r r u q r
p a s t r o n o m y e
e x o m o n t t b w v
n i l m a r i a r l o
u s s d e n b t a t l
m w t d c m s i m i u
b s i k p m b o t a t
r t c m l s s n p t i
a a e u i l k a i d o
y p h a s e s h n u n

Name ______________________ Date __________ Class ______________

CHAPTER 23

THE SOLAR SYSTEM

SECTION 23-1 Observing the Solar System
(pages 740–745)

This section describes the history of ideas about the solar system. It also explains the two factors that keep the planets in orbit around the sun.

▶ Wandering Stars (page 741)

1. What did the Romans name the five points of light that the Greeks called planets? ______________________________

____

▶ Greek Ideas: Earth at the Center (page 741)

2. In a geocentric system, what is the arrangement of planets? __________

____

3. What was Ptolemy's explanation for why the planets seemed to move at different speeds? ______________________________

____

____

▶ Copernicus's Idea: Sun at the Center (page 742)

4. A description of the solar system in which all the planets revolve around the sun is called a(n) ______________________.

5. In the 1500s, who developed a heliocentric explanation for the motion of the planets? ______________________________

▶ Galileo's Observations (page 742)

6. What were two observations that Galileo made through his telescope that supported the heliocentric model? ______________________

____

____

____

7. Circle the letter of whose ideas about the solar system are accepted today.

   a. Copernicus **b.** the Greeks **c.** Ptolemy **d.** the Romans

▶ Brahe and Kepler (pages 742–743)

8. What is an ellipse? ______________________

____

9. Complete the table about Brahe and Kepler.

Brahe and Kepler			
Observer	**Time**	**Identification**	**Accomplishment**
Tycho Brahe		Danish	
Johannes Kepler		German	

▶ Inertia and Gravity (pages 743–744)

10. What were the two factors Isaac Newton concluded that combined to keep the planets in orbit?

   a. ______________

   b. ______________

Name ______________________ Date __________ Class ______________

11. What is inertia? ______________________

____

____

12. Circle the letter of each statement that Newton made about the moon's orbit around Earth.

a. Earth pulls the moon toward it.

b. The moon keeps moving ahead because of gravity.

c. Earth curves away as the moon falls toward it.

d. Inertia keeps the moon moving ahead.

13. What does Figure 5 on page 744 show would happen if the force of gravity didn't pull the planet toward the sun? ______________________

____

____

14. Why are the planets in orbit around the sun? ______________________

____

____

▶ More to Discover (page 745)

15. Astronomers still use telescopes to study the solar system. How have they made even closer observations of the planets? ______________________

____

____

Reading Skill Practice

Writing a summary can help you remember the information you have read. When you write a summary, write only the most important points. On a separate sheet of paper, write a summary of the information in Section 23–1. Your summary should be shorter than the text on which it is based.

SECTION 23-2 The Sun (pages 746–750)

This section describes the sun's interior and its atmosphere. It also describes features on and above the sun's surface.

▶ The Sun's Interior (pages 746–747)

1. The sun's energy comes from the process called ______________.

2. What occurs in nuclear fusion? ______________________________

____

3. Where does nuclear fusion occur on the sun? ______________________

____

4. What are three products of the nuclear fusion that occurs on the sun?

a. ______________ b. ______________ c. ______________

▶ The Sun's Atmosphere (pages 747–748)

5. Complete the table about the layers of the sun's atmosphere.

The Sun's Atmosphere

Layer	Description	When Is It Visible?
Photosphere		
Chromosphere		
Corona		

6. The corona sends out a stream of electrically charged particles called

______________.

Name ______________________ Date ____________ Class ______________

▶ Features on the Sun (pages 748–750)

7. What are three features on or above the sun's surface?

a. ______________ b. ______________ c. ______________

8. Complete the table about features on the sun.

Features on the Sun	
Feature	**Description**
Sunspots	
Prominences	
Solar flares	

9. Short-term changes in climate on Earth may be related to

______________________.

10. When solar flares increase solar wind from the corona, what do they cause in Earth's upper atmosphere? ______________________

SECTION 23-3 The Inner Planets (pages 752–759)

This section describes the main characteristics of the four planets closest to the sun.

▶ Introduction (page 752)

1. Which planets are often called the terrestrial planets? ______________

____

____

2. What are two similarities among the inner planets? ______________

____

____

CHAPTER 23, The Solar System *(continued)*

3. Look at the table in Figure 10 on page 753. Rank the inner planets according to diameter. Rank the planet with the greatest diameter as *1.*

   ______ Mercury ______ Venus ______ Earth ______ Mars

4. Which planet rotates on its axis in about the same amount of time as Earth does? ________________

5. The drawing below shows the sun and the four inner planets. Label the inner planets according to their place in the solar system.

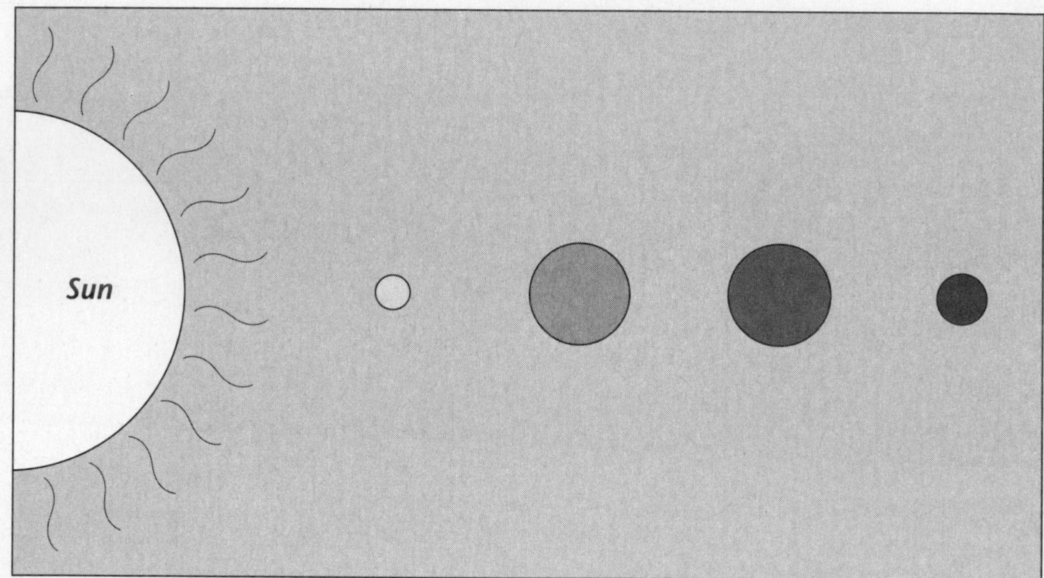

▶ Earth (pages 752–753)

6. Circle the letter of each sentence that is true about Earth.
   a. About 70 percent of its surface is covered with water.
   b. Its atmosphere extends about 1 kilometer above its surface.
   c. Most of the atmosphere is composed of oxygen gas.
   d. No other planet in the solar system has oceans like it.

7. What are the three main layers of Earth?

   a. ______________ b. ______________ c. ______________

8. What is Earth's dense inner core made of? ________________

9. How can studying Earth help scientists understand other planets?

____

____

____

▶ Mercury (page 754)

10. Is the following sentence true or false? Most of the gases Mercury once had in its atmosphere apparently escaped into space. ______________

11. Circle the letter of each sentence that is true about Mercury.
   a. Mercury's surface has many craters.
   b. Mercury has no moons.
   c. The interior of Mercury is composed mostly of the element mercury.
   d. Mercury is the planet closest to the sun.

12. Why does Mercury have a greater range of temperatures than any other planet? ______________________________

____

____

____

▶ Venus (pages 755–757)

13. Because Venus is often a bright object in the west after sunset, it is known as the ______________________.

14. Why is Venus sometimes called "Earth's twin"? ______________

____

15. Circle the letter of the gas that makes up most of the atmosphere of the planet Venus.
   a. oxygen
   b. nitrogen
   c. sulfuric acid
   d. carbon dioxide

16. Why is the rotation of Venus called retrograde rotation? ______________

____

____

17. Is the following sentence true or false? The atmosphere of Venus is so thick that it never has a sunny day. ______________

18. The trapping of heat by the atmosphere of Venus is called the ______________.

▶ Mars (pages 757–759)

19. Why is Mars called the "red planet"? ______________

____

____

20. The atmosphere on Mars is mostly ______________.

21. Is the following sentence true or false? There are no canals on Mars. ______________

22. Why do some regions on Mars look darker than others? ______________

____

____

____

23. Circle the letter of each sentence that is true about Mars.
   a. The rocks on Mars are covered with a rusty dust.
   b. Mars has seasons because it is tilted on its axis.
   c. Mars has many large oceans on its surface.
   d. Mars has giant volcanoes on its surface.

24. What are the two moons of Mars?

   a. ______________ **b.** ______________

Name ______________________ Date __________ Class ______________

SECTION 23-4 The Outer Planets (pages 760–767)

This section describes the main characteristics of the five planets farthest from the sun. It also explains how Pluto is different from the other planets.

▶ Structure of the Gas Giants (pages 760–761)

1. The first four outer planets do not have solid ______________.

2. Which four planets are known as the gas giants? ______________

____

3. What is the composition of the atmospheres of the gas giants? __________

____

____

____

4. Is the following sentence true or false? None of the gas giants has a solid surface, but all have a solid core. ______________

5. The drawing below shows the sun, the four inner planets, and the five outer planets. Label the outer planets according to their place in the solar system.

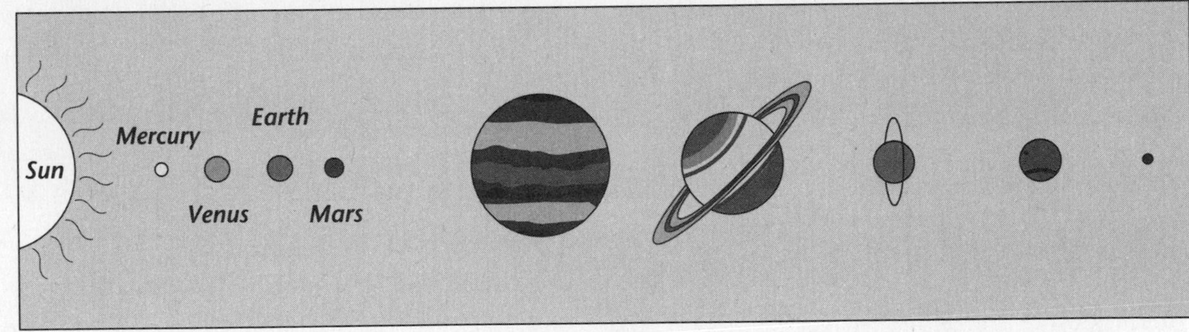

6. Why don't astronomers know much about the cores of the gas giants?

____

____

____

▶ Jupiter (pages 762–763)

7. Is the following sentence true or false? Jupiter's atmosphere is made up mainly of hydrogen and helium. ________________

8. What is the Giant Red Spot on Jupiter? ______________________________

____

____

9. Circle the letter of each sentence that is true about Jupiter.
   a. Jupiter's atmosphere contains many colorful bands.
   b. Jupiter's atmosphere is extremely thin.
   c. Jupiter has 17 moons revolving around it.
   d. Jupiter is the most massive planet in the solar system.

10. What are Jupiter's four largest moons?

    a. ________________ b. ________________

    c. ________________ d. ________________

11. Jupiter's moon Io is covered with ________________.

▶ Saturn (pages 763–764)

12. What are Saturn's rings made of? ______________________________

____

____

13. Is the following sentence true or false? Saturn has only 10 rings, although it looks like there are more. ________________

14. The largest of Saturn's 19 moons is called ________________.

▶ Uranus (page 765)

15. Why does Uranus look bluish? ______________________________

____

16. What made astronomer William Herschel famous in 1781? ________

17. How much larger is Uranus than Earth? ________

18. How is the rotation of Uranus unlike that of most of the other planets?

19. How many moons does Uranus have? ________

20. What are Uranus's five largest moons like? ________

▶ Neptune (page 766)

21. In the 1800s, why did astronomers predict that the planet Neptune would be discovered well before anyone had seen it? ________

22. Circle the letter of the sentence that explains how the Great Dark Spot was like the Great Red Spot.

a. Both formed from volcanoes.
b. Both formed on rings.
c. Both were probably storms.
d. Neither lasted long.

23. Is the following sentence true or false? Neptune's atmosphere is blue and nearly featureless. ________

24. Which is the largest of Neptune's eight moons? ________

▶ Pluto and Charon (page 767)

25. Is the following sentence true or false? Pluto is less than two thirds the size of Earth's moon. ______________

26. Why don't astronomers know much about Pluto and Charon? ______

____

____

27. Circle the letter of each sentence that is true about Pluto.

a. Its moon is more than half Pluto's size.

b. Both Pluto and Charon have gaseous surfaces.

c. Astronomers often consider Pluto and Charon a double planet.

d. The American astronomer Clyde Tombaugh discovered Pluto in 1930.

28. Why do some astronomers think Pluto should not be called a planet?

____

____

SECTION 23-5 Comets, Asteroids, and Meteors (pages 770-773)

This section describes the other objects in the solar system, including comets, asteroids, and meteors.

▶ Comets (pages 770–771)

1. What are comets? ______________________________

____

____

2. What are the three main parts of a comet?

a. ______________ **b.** ______________ **c.** ______________

3. How does a comet's tail form? ______________________________

____

____

4. Is the following sentence true or false? A comet's tail can be hundreds of millions of kilometers long. ______________

5. Who predicted that a comet would reappear in 1758? ______________

____

▶ Asteroids (page 772)

6. Objects revolving around the sun that are too small and too numerous to be called planets are called ______________.

7. Where is the asteroid belt? ______________________________

____

____

8. What happened when an asteroid collided with Earth 65 million years ago?

____

____

____

____

▶ Meteors (pages 772–773)

Match the term with its definition.

Term	Definition
______ 9. meteoroid	a. A meteoroid that has passed through the atmosphere and hit Earth's surface
______ 10. meteor	b. A chunk of rock or dust in space
______ 11. meteorite	c. A streak of light caused by the burning up of a meteoroid in the atmosphere

12. Where do meteoroids come from? ______________________________

____

13. The craters on the moon were caused by the impact of

______________.

SECTION 23-6 Is There Life Beyond Earth? (pages 774–777)

This section describes what conditions living things need to exist on Earth and explains why life might exist on Mars and Europa.

▶ Introduction (page 774)

1. Life other than that on Earth would be called ______________

______________.

▶ The "Goldilocks Conditions" (pages 774–775)

2. What are the three "Goldilocks conditions" that Earth has that life as we know it needs to exist?

   a. ____

   b. ____

   c. ____

▶ Life on Earth (page 775)

3. Where has life been found on Earth that suggests that life forms can exist that do not need the "Goldilocks conditions"? ______________

____

____

____

Name ______________________ Date __________ Class ______________

▶ Life on Mars? (pages 776–777)

4. Why is Mars the most obvious place to look for living things like those on Earth? ____

____

5. Why do scientists hypothesize that Mars may once have had the conditions needed for life to exist? ______________________________

____

____

____

6. A meteorite from Mars found in Antarctica in 1996 shows tiny shapes that look like ____________________.

7. Is the following sentence true or false? All scientists agree that the meteorite from Mars shows that life once existed on Mars.

____

8. What tested the soil of Mars for signs of life? ______________________

____

9. Is the following sentence true or false? Life has been discovered in Martian soil. ____________________

▶ Life on Europa? (page 777)

10. What suggests that there might be liquid water on Europa? ____________

____

____

____

11. Is the following sentence true or false? If there is liquid water on Europa, there might also be life. ____________________

Name ______________________ Date __________ Class ______________

WordWise

Answer the questions by writing the correct key terms in the blanks. Use the circled letters to find the hidden key term. Then write a definition for the hidden key term.

Clues

What is the middle layer of the sun's atmosphere?

_ ◯ _ _ _ _ _ _ _ ◯ _ _

What is an elongated circle, or oval shape, called?

_ _ ◯ _ _ _ _

What are the objects called that orbit the sun in a belt between Mars and Jupiter?

_ _ _ _ _ _ _ _ ◯ _ _

What is the spinning rotation of a planet from east to west called?

_ _ _ _ _ _ _ _ _ _   _ ◯ _ _ _ _ _ _

What is a description of the solar system in which all the planets revolve around Earth?

_ _ _ ◯ _ _ _ _ _ _

What is a chunk of rock or dust in space called?

_ _ _ ◯ _ _ _ _ _

What are reddish loops of gas that connect different parts of sunspot regions?

_ _ _ _ _ _ ◯ _ _ _ _

What are areas of gas on the sun that are cooler than the gases around them?

_ _ _ _ _ _ ◯ _

What is a stream of electrically charged particles sent out by the corona called?

_ _ _ _ ◯   _ ◯ _ _

What is the outer layer of the sun's atmosphere?

◯ _ _ _ _ _

Key Term: _ _ _ _ _ _ _ _ _ _ _ _

Definition: ____

____

Name ______________________ Date __________ Class ______________

CHAPTER 24

Stars, Galaxies, and the Universe

SECTION 24-1 Tools of Modern Astronomy (pages 784–790)

This section describes telescopes and other tools astronomers use to study the universe.

▶ Electromagnetic Radiation (page 785)

1. The light you see with your eyes is called ______________________.

2. What is electromagnetic radiation? ______________________

____

____

3. The distance between the crest of one wave and the crest of the next wave is called the ______________________.

4. A range of different wavelengths is called a(n) ______________________.

5. What colors form the spectrum of visible light? ______________________

____

6. What is the electromagnetic spectrum? ______________________

____

____

7. What wavelengths are included in the electromagnetic spectrum? ______

____

____

____

▶ Telescopes (pages 786–787)

8. What do most telescopes collect and focus? ______________________

____

____

9. What is a convex lens? ______________________

____

____

10. Complete the table about telescopes.

Telescopes	
Type	**Description**
Refracting telescope	
Reflecting telescope	
Radio Telescope	

11. What kind of telescope did Galileo use? ______________________.

12. The largest visible light telescopes are now all ______________________.

▶ Observatories (page 787)

13. A building that contains one or more telescopes is called a(n)

______________________.

14. Why have astronomers built the largest visible light telescopes on the tops of mountains? ______________________

____

____

Name ______________________ Date __________ Class ______________

▶ Satellites (page 788)

15. Why can the Hubble Space Telescope make images in visible light that are much better than images made by telescopes on Earth? ______________

____

____

____

▶ Spectrographs (pages 789–790)

16. What does a spectrograph do? ______________________

____

____

17. What are two kinds of information that astronomers can collect from stars by using spectrographs?

a. ______________________

b. ______________________

18. Is the following sentence true or false? Each element has a unique set of lines on a spectrum. ______________

19. How can astronomers infer which elements are found in a star? ______

____

____

____

20. Stars at different temperatures produce different ______________.

21. How can astronomers infer how hot a star is? ______________

____

____

____

SECTION 24-2 Characteristics of Stars (pages 793–799)

This section explains how astronomers measure distances to stars. It also describes how stars are classified.

▶ Introduction (page 793)

1. A cluster of stars, gases, and dust held together by gravity is called a(n)

______________.

2. What is the universe? ______________________________

____

3. Most of the universe is ______________.

▶ Distances to Stars (page 794)

4. Complete the table about units of distance.

Units of Distance	
Unit	**Definition**
Astronomical unit	
Light-year	

5. Is the following sentence true or false? The light-year is a unit of time.

____

▶ Measuring Distances to Stars (pages 794–795)

6. What is parallax? ______________________________

____

____

7. Circle the letter of what astronomers use parallax to measure the distance to.

   a. distant stars **b.** the sun **c.** the planets **d.** nearby stars

8. To measure parallax shift, astronomers look at the same star twice, when Earth is on different sides of the ________________.

▶ Classifying Stars (page 795)

9. What are the three main characteristics used to classify stars?

   a. ________________ **b.** ________________ **c.** ________________

▶ Sizes of Stars (page 796)

10. Stars that are much larger than the sun are called ________________.

11. Which kinds of stars are smaller than the sun?

    a. neutron star **b.** giant star **c.** supergiant star **d.** white dwarf star

▶ Color and Temperature of Stars (page 796)

12. What reveals a star's temperature? ______________________________

    ____

13. Circle the letter of what is revealed by the red color of the supergiant star called Betelgeuse.

    a. It is an extremely hot star. **b.** It is in a constellation.

    c. It is far away. **d.** It is a cool star.

▶ Brightness of Stars (pages 797–798)

14. The amount of light a star gives off is called its ________________.

15. Why does Rigel shine as brightly as Betelgeuse, even though Rigel is much smaller than Betelgeuse? ______________________________

    ____

    ____

    ____

16. How bright a star looks from Earth depends on what two factors?

a. ____

b. ____

17. Complete the table about the measurement of a star's brightness.

Brightness of Stars	
Measurement of Brightness	**Definition**
Apparent magnitude	
Absolute magnitude	

18. Is the following sentence true or false? The closer a star is to Earth, the brighter it is. ______________

19. What two things must an astronomer find out in order to calculate a star's absolute magnitude?

a. ____

b. ____

▶ The Hertzsprung-Russell Diagram (pages 798–799)

20. The diagram that shows the relationship between the surface temperature and the brightness of stars is called the

______________________________.

21. Look at the Hertzsprung-Russell diagram in Figure 10 on page 799. Write what is measured on each of the two axes of the diagram.

x-axis (horizontal axis): ______________________________

y-axis (vertical axis): ______________________________

22. An area on the Hertzsprung-Russell diagram that runs from the upper left to the lower right and includes more than 90 percent of all stars is called the ______________________.

Name ______________________ Date __________ Class __________

23. Circle the letter of each sentence that is true based on the Hertzsprung-Russell diagram.

a. The sun is a main-sequence star.

b. White dwarfs are brighter than supergiants.

c. Rigel is hotter than Betelgeuse.

d. Polaris is brighter than the sun.

Reading Skill Practice

A flowchart can help you remember the order of steps in a process. On a separate sheet of paper, create a flowchart that describes the steps that astronomers use to measure the distance to stars, as described on pages 794–795. The first step in your flowchart should be: Astronomers look at a star when Earth is on one side of the sun. For more information about flowcharts, see page 833 in the Skills Handbook of your textbook.

SECTION 24-3

Lives of Stars (pages 802–806)

This section explains how the life of a star begins. It also explains what determines how long a star lives and what happens when a star runs out of fuel.

▶ Introduction (page 802)

1. A neutron star that gives off pulses of radio waves is called a(n) ______________.

▶ Studying the Lives of Stars (page 802)

2. Since astronomers can't study a single star for billions of years, how do they know that stars go through stages in their lives? ______________

____

____

▶ A Star Is Born (page 803)

3. A large amount of gas and dust spread out in an immense volume is called a(n) ________________.

4. Is the following sentence true or false? All stars begin their lives as part of nebulas. ________________

5. The earliest stage of a star's life is called a(n) ________________.

6. Describe how a star is born. ____

____

____

▶ Lifetimes of Stars (page 803)

7. Circle the letter of the factor that determines how long a star lives.

   a. its mass **b.** its brightness **c.** its volume **d.** its temperature

8. Is the following sentence true or false? Stars with more mass last longer than stars with less mass. ________________

▶ Deaths of Stars (pages 804–806)

9. Complete the table by writing the definition of each term.

Deaths of Stars	
Term	**Definition**
White dwarf	
Black dwarf	
Supernova	
Neutron star	
Black hole	

10. Use the information in *Exploring the Lives of the Stars* on page 805 to complete the flowchart.

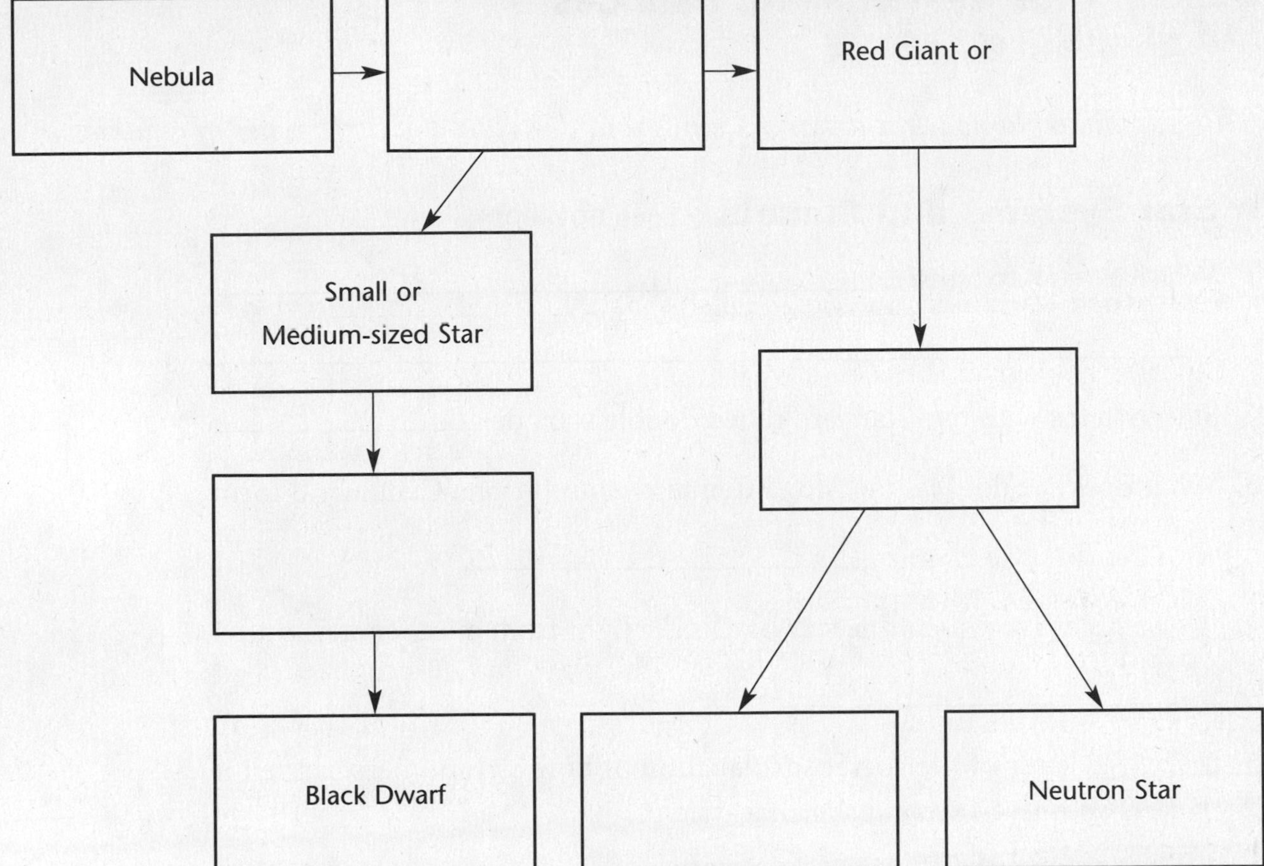

11. How do astronomers think the sun may have begun? ______________

____

____

12. Because no form of radiation can ever get out of a black hole, how can astronomers detect where black holes are? ______________

____

____

____

13. A distant galaxy with a black hole at its center is called a(n) ______________.

SECTION 24-4

Star Systems and Galaxies

(pages 807–810)

This section explains what a star system is and describes the three types of galaxies.

▶ Star Systems and Planets (pages 807–809)

1. What are star systems? ______________________________

____

2. Star systems with two stars are called double stars or ______________.

3. What does the double star Alpha Centauri A and Alpha Centauri B form with Proxima Centauri? ______________________

4. A star system in which one star blocks the light from another star is a(n) ______________________.

5. Circle the letter of the correct explanation of how astronomers can tell if there is an unseen second star in a system.

a. They observe the effects of its gravity.

b. They measure the parallax of the second star.

c. They send a probe to the second star.

d. They observe its supernova.

6. How did astronomers deduce that the star called 51 Pegasi has a planet revolving around it? ______________________________

____

▶ Galaxies (pages 809–810)

7. The galaxy in which our solar system is located is called the ______________________.

8. How many galaxies are there in the universe? ______________

9. On the drawing of the Milky Way Galaxy below, place a dot and write a label that shows where the sun is located.

Milky Way Galaxy

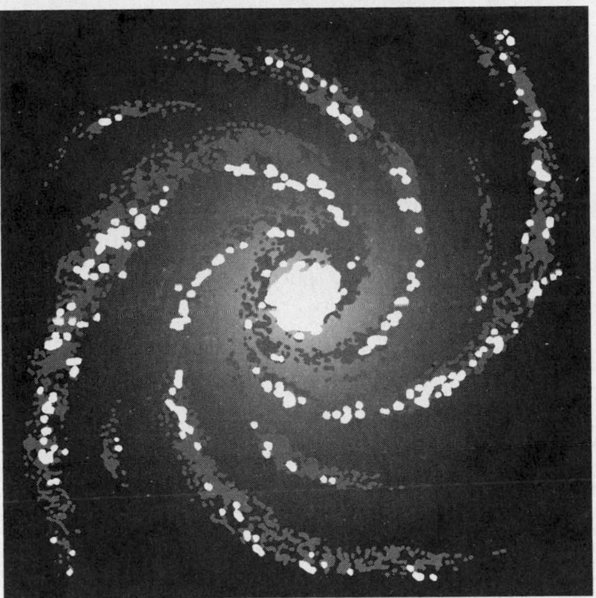

10. Complete the table about types of galaxies.

Types of Galaxies	
Type	**Description of Shape**
Spiral galaxies	
Elliptical galaxies	
Irregular galaxies	

11. For each galaxy below, write the type that it is.

Milky Way Galaxy: ______________________

Large Magellanic Cloud: ______________________

12. Circle the letter of each sentence that is true about galaxies.

a. Ellipitical galaxies contain only new stars.

b. There is lots of gas and dust between the stars in the Milky Way Galaxy.

c. The center of the Milky Way Galaxy is about 25,000 light years from the sun.

d. All galaxies have regular shapes.

SECTION 24-5 History of the Universe
(pages 811–814)

This section explains how astronomers think the universe and the solar system formed.

▶ Moving Galaxies (pages 811–812)

1. To study how and when the universe formed, what kind of information do astronomers use? ______________________________

____

____

2. Is the following sentence true or false? The further away a galaxy is from us, the faster it is moving away from us. ______________

3. How is the universe like rising raisin bread dough? ______________

____

____

____

____

▶ The Big Bang Theory (pages 812–813)

4. The initial explosion that resulted in the formation and expansion of the universe is called the ______________.

5. When did the big bang occur? ______________________________

____

6. From what can astronomers infer approximately how long the universe has been expanding? ______________________________

____

Name ______________________ Date __________ Class __________

▶ Formation of the Solar System (pages 813–814)

7. Our solar system formed about ______________________.

8. How did our solar system form? ______________________

____

____

____

9. What events led to the birth of the sun? ______________________

____

____

____

____

____

▶ The Future of the Universe (page 814)

10. Describe two possibilities of what will happen to the universe in the future.

 a. ______________________

 ____

 ____

 ____

 ____

 b. ______________________

 ____

 ____

 ____

 ____

WordWise

Solve the clues by filling in the blanks with key terms from Chapter 24. Then write the numbered letters in the correct order to find the hidden message.

Clues	Key Terms
The earliest stage of a star's life	_ _ _ _ _ _ _ _ _ (1)
The remains of a massive star pulled into a small volume by gravity	_ _ _ _ _ _ _ _ _ (2)
An instrument that breaks the light from an object into colors and photographs the resulting spectrum	_ _ _ _ _ _ _ _ _ _ _ _ (3)
All of space and everything in it	_ _ _ _ _ _ _ _ (4)
A tiny star that remains after a supernova	_ _ _ _ _ _ _ _ _ _ _ (5)
The explosion that formed the universe	_ _ _ _ _ _ _ (6)
A pattern of stars in the sky	_ _ _ _ _ _ _ _ _ _ _ _ _ (7)
The explosion of a dying giant or supergiant star	_ _ _ _ _ _ _ _ _ (8)
A galaxy that has a pinwheel shape	_ _ _ _ _ _ _ _ _ _ _ _ (9)
A building that contains one or more telescopes	_ _ _ _ _ _ _ _ _ _ _ (10)
A device used to detect radio waves from objects in space	_ _ _ _ _ _ _ _ _ _ _ _ _ _ (11)
The apparent change in position of an object when you look at it from different places	_ _ _ _ _ _ _ _ (12)
A distant galaxy with a black hole at its center	_ _ _ _ _ _ (13)

Hidden Message

_ _ _   _ _ _   _ _   _   _ _ _ _ .

1 2 3   4 5 6   7 8   9   10 11 12 13